Ian

A soulsister on life's journey

Love from

Alise

A Songbird

whose Name

is Love

ALISON STRANDBERG

To Pat

with much love

from Sheila x

Christmas 2016

Acknowledgments

I would like to say thankyou to all the people who have stuck by me throughout the years of writing the story and for encouraging me all the time. A very special thanks goes to Thorn Steafel as my book midwife, and to Jo Abbott for lending me the beautiful cover.

In my heart of a thousand sorrows
dwells a songbird, whose name is love.
Open the casement of your heart
and allow her to fly in.
The songbird sees into the hearts of darkness,
wherein dwell fear and self doubt.
Each pure note from her voice
sends a crystal tone into those hearts
and melts the darkness.

Cecile

It is the summer of 1497. I am very happy, for today I have met the one who is to be my all. I do not blaspheme when I say this as I know the Lord, who loves us all, understands and condones what I am doing and being. What is love I ask myself? What is it to love another human being? It is to be so pure in spirit and so filled with the joy of being and the wonderment for the emotion, which can be between two souls.

My story is a short one, but not uncomplicated. My name is Cecile de Martin and I am seventeen years old. I was born in the village of Saint Martin on the banks of the Loire, not far from the community of Fontevraud, where the great Abbaye de Fontevraud lies. My childhood was a happy one and privileged, as my father had land and enough wealth to make life easy to live. We were never a close family my brothers, sister and I and I was always a little different. It was my mother, alone, who understood me and stood by me when fate dealt me blows in life. My siblings did not understand the abilities I possessed and found them odd and strangely frightening. My mother, who was a very wise woman, saw my future as being in a safe place where I would not be harmed for my powers. If I was hidden under a nun's habit, who would find it strange that I could talk directly with God and have my questions answered.

It was not with sorrow I was to leave my home and to become one of the nuns in the Abbaye de Fontevraud. My father was not without influence in the area and he was able to procure a place for me in the convent when I had reached the age of fourteen. The Abbaye was known far and wide as a place of great beauty, as well as a place to do with riches and high standing. Those great kings and queens who lay buried within the Abbaye would look upon these scurrying nuns and monks perhaps as lesser beings when in this world, but once passed over to the other world, would see what peace and solitude meant to the initiated and understand their need to hide away.

My entering into the life of the Abbaye was not altogether free from difficulties. To be accepted into such a distinguished Order was not an easy thing, but the fact that my father was persuasive was of use. He did, however, have to wait some time before the decision to accept me as a novice was taken. My path in life came about mainly due to the compassion and sincerity of the Mother Abbess, who was in charge of the running of the Abbaye de Fontevraud. As a nun, she was very fair, kind, compassionate and with an inner strength and will that carried her forward at all times. As a woman and as a fellow human being, she was as precious to me as a rare jewel or the egg found hiding underneath the hen when there is no more food to be found on the farm. To say that I looked up to this woman would be too little. I owe everything to her for the years of happiness in the Abbaye de Fontevraud.

My first meeting with the Mother Abbess was filled with peace. I felt an affinity with this person immediately and knew that she alone understood my inner feelings and my need to seek solitude from the cruelties of the world outside. Her path may have been a similar one. Such knowledge never passed between us in words, but our souls understood each other at once. She saw in me a gentleness and purity, which others may only have seen and wanted to make fun of, because of their fear of it. She lifted my heart and showed me the way ahead and I was so grateful at last to have found my place. That I was only fourteen and unaware of the ways of the Abbaye and convent life did not seem to perturb her once her decision had been made. She knew that this was the path set out for me and she had been placed there to help me. Sometimes in life we meet people who we know so well it is almost perturbing, but only if we do not seek the answers to why inside our hearts.

The one thing that made my heart sore was leaving my beloved mother, but I knew that she was always with me within my heart and that she would always nurture her love for me until her dying day. It was a great offering for her to give me up to the church, but she knew it was what she had to do.

My life became easier as the days and weeks passed and I slipped into the ways of the Abbaye. From dawn to dusk I was busy and followed a strict regime where prayers and duties were very important. I enjoyed being in such a place of reverence and felt the love of God permeate the whole place. It was not such as His love can be felt in the great outdoors, when man is at one with nature, but it was more demure and contemplative. I relished the possibility of being able to be at prayer so much for to speak with my God and the Lord Jesus, was to me a way of life. I was perhaps a very unusual child, but it was a place where I really wanted to be.

The Abbaye was a beautiful place and rather unusual in that it combined both a nunnery and a monastery within its walls. The two areas did not have much contact, but it was the Mother Abbess who dealt with the running of both. It did not always go down well with the monks that they were governed by a woman, but as she was such a fair person it was easier for them to accept. We lived our daily lives separately, only coming together on feast days, saints' days and the days in the church calendar, which were especially celebrated. It was not that we were not to speak with each other, but the Mother Abbess knew what may befall us if the circumstances between man and woman evolved into those in the lives of men and women without the Abbaye. There was, however, one place within the Abbaye where nuns and monks did meet and exchange words of wisdom. This was in the hospital, or the Saint Lazare de la Sacre Coeur, where sick people and lepers were cared for. There was a flourishing use of herbs and herbal remedies in the care of these people and I felt my calling to this place almost immediately

It was not for me, however, to decide where I would be placed and I knew that my duties lay in serving God in prayer in those first months. I was but a novice and had to learn from the knowledge of those who knew more and had suffered more. Suffering is only the ability to accept what is given to one and to use the experience that may be of great burden in some way to show appreciation of God. My sufferings had not been great and I had to learn. It was not too great a suffering to have had my hair cut off, the hair, which my mother so lovingly brushed every day and bound up into plaits, which resembled the ears of corn, which grew in my father's fields. I wore the coarse habit of a nun, but to me it was never a burden to wear such a garment, as I had no need to show what God had given me on the outside as some enhancement for the whole of me. I knew that my beauty and the beauty of all others permeates the whole body and shines from the soul's bearers of joy; the eyes.

God had given me one other great gift. It was the gift of song. From my very earliest memories I was always singing, even if it was some tuneless childish melody. Sometimes I had to be admonished by my parents as I could not stop "making a noise" as they called it. I had so much joy within me I had to make it come out in some way. The Abbaye was not the place for noise or bustle and most of our days passed in virtual silence, but the silence from outside did not upset me or trouble me as inside my head there was always a bubbling or a talking or a singing going on. I felt almost encased in a cartridge of oak where nothing could get in and I could keep all this happiness within me. It could, however, reach out to others so that it could also touch their souls, but I never felt afraid to be touched by their thoughts. My own little world was so safe and so secure that I never envisaged that there was a word of evil around me.

I was to sing in the Abbaye when the nuns and monks celebrated great days of note. It was so wonderful to be able to lift people's hearts just by allowing the joy to soar out and to be heard. I sang for the Lord Jesus, Mother Mary and my God and I praised them as highly as was possible for me. I never stopped thanking God for allowing me to possess this wonderful gift.

As I became more at one with my life in the Abbaye, I became acquainted with the other nuns who were with me there. We passed our days mostly in silence, but there were times when words could be exchanged and also feelings. Not all of the nuns who were within the Abbaye were there for the same purpose as I was. Some had sought refuge from outer circumstances and saw the Abbaye as a safe place, while others were there only to be hidden away from their families, or the need for them to be married off, where they were one in a long line of sisters. Abbey life was very, very hard for them, for the commitment to Our Lord and Lady Mary was not easy for them at first. The love of their earthly dear ones was too great at first to let go and many unhappy moments were spent during their first weeks and months. I could understand how they were feeling and I sought to help them to see the beauty and excitement of the place we had chosen or had had chosen for us. It made me happy to be able to show them the pathway, which was theirs to follow.

I came to know one young nun better than all the others. Like me she was following a pathway, which her heart had shown her and it was always the right place for her to be. Her name was Columbine and she came from the south from a family, who were involved with the church, so her pathway had been set out for her from first babyhood. She was so pure and so free from vice and she always strove to exalt others in her vicinity. I loved her as though she was my sister and felt I had always known her. Our lives were to become intertwined in a strange and sad way, but our love for each other was never to cease. When I learned the names of the herbs and plants later on in my life, I was to discover that the name Columbine comes from the dove, which represents peace. Her whole being surrounded all who walked with her, with a calming blanket of peace and tranquillity. When friendships are tried and tested it is always the first areas we learn to love about another person, which are the ones to be tried the hardest. It is a feat to be able to hold on to these strings of hope and to hold them above one's head not to be pulled down into the mire. The strings which surrounded Columbine were never ever tarnished throughout all our trials.

Thus it was I spent my first years at the Abbaye de Fontevraud learning the lessons I was to learn. The love of those whom I cared for and the love of nature and the love of God were the three things, which were to be the most important in my life. I learned patience, tolerance, acceptance and compassion. I learned about fear, of not being afraid and of using fear to learn lessons. I learned all these things and more. I loved the place I had been led to and I was at peace with myself, with the world and the Lord. I was to look back on this period as a tranquil and happy time, but I never regretted the way the path led me.

* * *

After many days and months in service to my Lord Jesus, I was to be allowed to serve Him in another way. It had been my desire to help others when I first entered the Abbaye, but I had first to be prepared for this mission and to know enough about myself and my ability to help and know the pain of others, before it was right for me to take on this purpose. It is only possible to deal with another's pain if we first learn to know our own.

I was a very lucky child and I knew of little pain before being accepted into the Abbaye and thus it was more difficult for me to be accepted as a helper of others. The Mother Abbess did, however, realise my desire to be of service to those in pain and she was able to teach me lessons in that which I had to know of other people's pain. She noticed in me a quality, whereby I felt other people's feelings and could relate to how emotions bubbled up from within. In being of service to God, I could also be of service to those who did not have such a fortunate life.

There were many people who came to the Abbaye de Fontevraud to seek help for their ailments and many of those were lepers. God had given these souls great strength in order to live their lives in this way, for to live as a leper is very, very hard indeed. One must suffer the physical pain and discomfort, but one must also suffer the hatred and loathing of others who would fear you for looking and being different. The fear of becoming a leper can alter the natural love within oneself toward another human being and causes people to be afraid of their fellow man, lest they should become like them. I never feared these people, but instead felt I must help them and alleviate their suffering.

The Saint Lazare de la Sacre Coeur, the hospital, was situated aside from the rest of the Abbaye, partly to keep those who suffered from a terrible disease away from the other inhabitants and partly to allow them solitude from the fear of others. It was a beautiful place set within a garden, which was tended by the nuns and monks who were knowledgeable in the use of herbs to alleviate pain and suffering. Plants and flowers, which contained special powers to be used to make potions, potages and poultices were grown and the smell of the different herbs and flowers was very pleasing and comforting. I can still see the colours of these beautiful plants merging and undulating and thrusting their heads high into the sky in order to seek the sun, which provided them with the life giving force to heal. The scents, which pervaded the air around the Saint Lazare were heady and aromatic; lavender, thyme, comfrey, love-in-a-mist, rosebay willow herb, rosemary and columbine are all names, which are embedded in my memories.

It was not my request, which led me to the herb gardens of the Saint Lazare hospital. Instead, having learned many lessons through prayer and solitude, I was asked to go along with one of my fellow nuns, who was to help with the gathering of certain herbs for the treatment of an ailment for one of our sisters in the Abbaye. I was to help to carry the plants back to the Abbaye and to assist her on her mission. Little did I know that this occasion was to change my life for ever.

We set out in the early morning after prayers and devotions as it was the most appropriate time of the day to gather the flowers and the herbs. We went to the garden where the apothecary was situated, where the monks, who had great experience in creating the right blend of plants and herbs. had their office. It must have taken these men many, many years to build up the knowledge they had and to be able to extract their knowledge to treat each individual ailment. Sister Marie-Claire, who knew the elderly monk, who was in charge of the collection of the herbs, led us to the rear of the garden. We were to pick columbine, as this was used to alleviate stomach pains and cramps. It was to be mixed with several other plants in order to make a mixture, which could be drunk.

I had been in the Abbaye for three years by this time and had only encountered the monks during festivals and feast days, when we would come together in worship. It seemed strange to be communicating with a man again and meeting face to face. There were some nuns, who helped out in the apothecary, but mostly, it was men who dealt with the manufacturing of the medicines. The nuns then dealt with caring for the sick and using the medicines and potions. Novices, both nuns and monks were, however, able to help with the actual picking of the herbs and plants and it was through this I met the one who was to mean more to me than life.

I was at work in the garden and could feel the sun beating down on my cloaked head. It was early summer, but the sun was already high in the sky and the heat could be felt. It was such a wonderful feeling as I had loved the sun and its power to brighten all that it encompassed. When I was a little child, I would scurry around on the farm, tripping through the fields, lifting my skirts, turning and winding and dancing to a rhythm, which came from within. I called these dances "sun dances", as they made me feel so full of life as though the sun was reaching down and filling me with its love and life and asking me -no begging me – to be as happy as I could possibly be. On my knees in the garden of the Saint Lazare I once again remembered the power of this little ritual and I longed to be able to dance the dances I once had danced as a child.

Thus it was that I stood up, looked around to make sure I was alone for a moment, while Sister Marie-Claire conversed within the apothecary with the Brother of the apothecary, and raised my arms, which had been revealed for the first time in three years. I knew I should not be indulging in such childish whims, but the joy and the uplift I felt made me believe that Jesus would never disapprove of such behaviour. As I was doing this I suddenly became aware that I was not alone, but I knew that whoever was watching me was not Brother Vermont or Sister Marie-Claire, for if it were to have been either, they would have chastised me for my frivolity. I could feel the eyes of someone else watching me and I knew I had to turn around to see these eyes. As I turned I saw a young monk a short distance behind me who was in the process of bringing herbs to the apothecary. He had stopped in the process having seen my antics. On turning around, my eyes met the bluest eyes I had ever seen in my life. They were the colour of the sky and the sea; they were the blue of every colour which nature allows to be and they changed and altered as the sun hit them. My eyes gazed into these eyes – brown to blue – and I saw within the most beautiful soul and I knew right away the love that I felt for this person was so great it engulfed me and tore me away from the moment I was alive in. My soul had seen a soul from within and I loved this other soul as I never have nor ever will again.

It was to my fortune that I was suddenly called upon by Sister Marie-Claire and I was forced to look away from these beautiful eyes, before I became too immersed. I jumped up and ran to the apothecary and was then taken over by the tasks I had to carry out. The young monk did not appear again as he had been met by another monk on his way into the apothecary and had gone on his way again. My heart was so filled with love throughout the day I sought the solitude of prayer and meditation that I may be alone with my feelings and the joy that was taking over my whole being. Never did it occur to me that what I felt was wrong. It was as I had felt with the "sun dance". God would want me to be filled with joy and love for the sun and for his creatures. Why then should I not be allowed to feel this love within me for what was yet only another one of his creatures? I was too naïve then and too believing to be able to see the pathway ahead onto which these emotions could lead me.

I was not to return to the garden of the Saint Lazare, for other tasks were set out for me during these hot and sultry summer months. I was, however, given some instruction in the care of the sick and felt that I was being prepared for work in this area. The fact that I never saw the young monk during this time did not dissuade me nor quell the feelings inside. Instead, the time I had to dwell on them made me even stronger and I was so sure that some day I would see those eyes once again. The opportunity was to be given to me at the celebrations at Lammas to praise God for the harvest and for all the wondrous beauties the earth offered up to us who live on this earth.

In the days previous to the Lammas feast day there was much activity within the Abbaye. Produce, which had been grown within the grounds of the Abbaye, was gathered in order to be displayed during worship on the actual feast day. There was much to be displayed, as the Abbaye grounds stretched for some distance and encompassed many different areas of the countryside. Farm produce, such as wheat sheaves, eggs, vegetables, fruits, as well as herbs, plants, birch and beech twigs, foliage for the floors of the Abbaye and wood to be used in the making of the sculptures to enhance the beauty of the Abbaye in the uplift for the eye to worship the Lord God on High. As the monastery was also part of the Abbaye there was some movement among the monks to and fro to the main Abbaye building where worship would take place. I thought, perhaps, I would see the eyes of the young monk again, but it was not to be. I was never, however, discouraged, as I knew that as likely it was that I was a child of God, that I would gaze on them once more.

The Mother Abbess had recognized in me my love of music and song and I had been fortunate in being allowed to use my voice in singing God's praises at worship in times of special service to God, but only when it was fitting and only when the nuns of the order were present. This time she recognized the occasion as one where I would use the gift I had to glorify God in song and to lift the souls of the others who would listen to me. I was to spend many hours in practice for this great event as the Abbaye de Fontevraud was renowned far and wide and it was not anyone who was chosen to praise God through song. To me it was such a joy to be able to lift my voice and to be heard and to allow others to be touched by the emotion this could bring about, as the hearts and souls of those around opened and rejoiced. I was never afraid to stand alone and open my heart in joy and praise, for I sang for Mother Mary, the Lord Jesus and the Saints and mostly for God Himself.

On the morning of the feast day of Lammas I awakened as usual, but with a tingling in my body I had never felt before. I felt as though the whole of my being was on fire and had been lit up from within, but the sensation was not unpleasant, but instead invigorating and very pleasing. I did not then realise what it meant, but I was to understand as the days flew past and made their mark on time. I was anxious to be up and about and doing what I had to do to complete the tasks of the day. As usual we followed the limitations we as Sisters of Jesus, were led to in our daily lives, but I felt that the time would not approach quickly enough for me to stand before the hushed Abbaye and sing for all my worth in order to show my love and joy for my having been made such a privileged being.

The light was beginning to dull as we took our places in the Abbaye for the worshipping of Lammas and for thanksgiving to God. It was always a beautiful season to me the change from summer to autumn, but from now on it would have an even more important meaning. The last rays of the sun shone into the lit Abbaye as I moved forward to take my place with the other nuns and monks who were to sing for the congregation.. It was rather strange to think that for once nun and monk were equal and could share the same space in a confined area. It made my heart glad as I never had really understood the reasons why man and woman had to be separated from one another. The music, which reached my ears from the chanting of the monks, was truly beautiful and so fitting in such a holy place. The building was very old and great men and women lay around us; people who had been greatly looked up to. Now it was their privilege to lie in their stone coffins and listen to the tones of beauty, which surrounded the whole building.

As I walked towards the spot where I was to stand, I made the sign of the cross and felt that Jesus was with me and would help me to sing as well as I could. As I opened my mouth to sing, my gaze fell upon the congregation gathered before me, but one person held my gaze more than any other. There in the congregation I saw again these beautiful blue eyes and this time I saw them watching my own eyes and I could decipher in them, even at a distance, the emotion, which was behind them. I could feel the love, which was sent towards my own being from the eyes of this man, who looked upon me with such gentleness and such love it made my heart move. I sang for him as if he alone was present in that great cathedral; as if he symbolized the love I felt for God and for His Son and for all His creatures on earth. My heart was so full of emotion, it was almost fit to break, but with true joy not with sorrow.

The emotion I felt in that moment stayed with me in the following days and months of my life. Not for one second did the feeling of overwhelming love ever leave me. It was as if God had sent me an angel on earth to show me that he really did exist. That I did not understand that such feelings were wrong of me to experience never entered into my head. I knew that I loved and loved so deeply, I could never let the love go. To nurture thoughts of guilt or remorse did not ever occur to me.

My life moved on from that day. I was to change duties and tasks for different ones. I was to enter the garden of the Saint Lazare, but this time not just once, but many times. I was to become a novice of the hospital and was put under the instruction of a nun by the name of Celestine. She was a rather thickset and sturdy person, but her heart was filled with goodness and the earthiness, which showed in her physical body belied the spirituality within. She was a very caring and warm person and she taught me a great deal.

My first meeting with the lepers was to be one of joy rather than uneasiness and fear. I followed in the footsteps of Sister Celestine as she moved amongst those who were sick and infirm in the hospital and felt their eyes watching me in the hope that some cure would alleviate their sufferings and put right the wrongs they felt the world had dealt them. We were to spend many hours in the day tending these soul and helping with physical tasks, such as bandaging, laying poultices of herbs and plants on their maimed bodies, touching their hands or shoulders and holding them as if to give them the life force, which came from God. It was often in these moments when we were at one, the sufferer and the healer, that I felt total contentment and belief in the reasons why we are sent to Earth. If it was meant that we would learn lessons on our paths through life, how more fitting could it be that we would give of each others' experiences; the one who felt the greatest pain and the one who administered hope to the doomed. To realize that we each possessed part of a puzzle and that no part was greater than the other, was to me the most important thing I had ever learned. What great knowledge and understanding God must possess in allowing us to face our fears and to face them with a positivity which can only promote love.

There are times in one's life when a picture forms in front of one's eyes as though the hand of a mighty artist from on high is painting the story of one's life. Beautiful hues and stark, gloomy colours illuminate the picture in different areas. All we see is a muddle of colours, visions and a feeling of knowing something about this special picture. If it were a tapestry, we would look upon the threads first from the front of the weave and then from the rear and it would make no sense. What we do not know is that we weave a picture all our own through our own feelings, deeds and misdeeds. It is only when it is too late we make a realisation that we had a choice and at important times in life we were guided towards our goal. How I wished later, that I had listened to my guiding light in those happy days so far apart from what was to be. This was, however, my choice and in judging myself I judge my God who knows me and loves me and accepts my flaws and lack of trust. My picture was a beautiful one to Him no matter how it appeared, for it was my struggle to achieve what I once knew I had to achieve. If it fell short of the mark, then it was I, and only I, who would judge myself and wish that events had taken another turn.

The Quickening

Gentleness is love; love is the key, which turns the lock, which holds the pain inside. There is gentleness in the touch of a human hand on another human being, but the gentleness in the touch of a thought or feeing conveyed to another is even greater. The healing that is done from hour to hour in caring for those who are not whole, or who are sickly and infirm calls for the ultimate gentleness, which God allows us to experience. I learned much about love in its many forms in the months which followed Lammas. My soul had learned the greatest love a human being could feel for another and although it was not even reciprocated at close hand I knew that

I was as beloved as I in turn loved.

My pathway to the garden of the Saint Lazare hospital led through the cloisters of the Abbaye and out into an open courtyard, before turning to the left and following the path, which entered into the herb garden by way of a gate, which was reached by three steps. I enjoyed my free time on my way from the cloisters to the garden, as it gave me time to consider and to contemplate. I was at this time allowed to follow my pathway by myself as I was entrusted with the task I was to carry out by the Sisters in the Order and by the Mother Abbess herself.

It was en route to the Saint Lazare hospital that I was to encounter the young monk for the third time. I had set out as usual to follow my path via the herb garden to collect the herbs I needed for poultices and had just left the cloisters to enter the open courtyard, when I saw a figure hurrying towards me from the direction of the monastery. This building lay a little way aside from the buildings of the nunnery within the main building and thus it was not often we had contact with the monks within this area. He seemed a little flustered and was intent on his mission with head bowed down and with his mind set out on the direction his body would take him. I did not at first realise whose the figure was and he came so close so as almost to bump into me. I hastened out of his way and only then did he look up and I saw that it was he whom I dwelt on in my mind in every waking moment. I had never been so close to him before and my feelings were very close to the surface, for I could not stop myself from letting out a gasp as he looked up. I could see in his eyes, that he was as startled as I, but he was clever at disguising this fact as he looked up, but my heart felt a jolt, which passed between us both.

My feet would not move from the spot; it felt as though they had been nailed to the earth and it was not possible for me to move away. The young monk looked at me with consternation and pure emotion in his eyes. It was as difficult for him to remove himself from the situation we found ourselves in. As we stood there, as if in a frozen manner, like two statues bewitched, he touched my hand lightly and asked if I should not be going my way and if he could aid me with anything on that mission. I thanked him kindly and replied that I was on my way to the Saint Lazare hospital to carry out my tasks with the lepers. I knew that it was wrong of me to converse with a monk as much as it would have been wrong of me to converse with one of the sisters unless the words which passed between us were of benefit to my task. It felt as though I never wanted his voice to stop, as if I wanted the sound to merge into my mind and into my soul for ever so that I could bring it out at any time in the future to savour and to have as comfort and solace.

Much as I would have wanted to stay in the moment for eternity, my earthly knowledge of how to react made me move away uttering a thank you as

I scuttled in the direction of the garden. My heart beat as if it were fit to burst and as if it were moving out of my body. I rearranged my habit in order that no one would see how my heart beat, for it felt as if anyone who looked on me would notice. I gathered myself together in the herb garden and made my way slowly to the hospital to carry out my daily tasks. I only wished that I could have stayed with the soul whom I loved, in order that I may make his acquaintance and talk to him as I wished to talk to him. I knew that the communication between our two souls was already fully developed and that I could read his thoughts as he could mine, but the desire to be in his presence and around his being compelled me to wish for another meeting with him. I knew deep in my heart that this was only the beginning of an episode that would be played out by the hands of those greater than us mortals. The strings are there for us to grasp at and we, and only we, propel ourselves in the way we want the strings to move.. Those greater beings of light, who watch us in our travails, look down and hold us up as the strings tangle and cross and sometimes realign, but never ever do they shake their fingers at us in scorn. They do, instead, radiate their love and compassion for us and allow us, ourselves, to make mistakes as we see it or perhaps not mistakes, but differences in the flow of life. We are always in the flow of life if we wish, but sometimes we prefer to cling blindly to the rocks in the current.

Walking through the cloisters and the courtyard caused me once again to make the acquaintance of the young monk some weeks later. It was not a coincidence that we met there, as he was en route to his daily task just as I was. We looked at each other with open eyes this time, as the pathways of the soul were now truly open. Whether we wanted to observe the rules of the Order or not was not the question any longer. We knew within our hearts that what was to be was to be. This time we stopped and smiled and he asked how it was with the lepers and if my hands were as gentle with them as he felt my hand to be when he touched me that first time. I felt myself in need of words from his lips, that I may know of his business in his daily life and he told me what he had not told any other than those who led him in his tasks. He followed this pathway every day as he was the keeper of the Holy Doves of the Abbaye de Fontevraud. The doves represented the Holy Spirit and had once been blessed by Saint Benedict as the species that for him represented the way towards God; white for purity, the bird as the symbol of freedom and light with its ability to reach to the heavens. Its outstretched wings portrayed the ability to enfold and encompass the hearts of men, who would look upon its beauty in wonder and see in the dove the Spirit of God Himself. That this young man was the custodian and keeper of those doves made him even more special in my heart, for he seemed as pure as the doves themselves.

Parting was not difficult this time, for now I knew our paths would cross many times in the future. We followed the same ways at the same time, so we were to meet with ease and without fearing that it had been previously thought out. I learned that the doves, which he tended, were kept in a small garden, which led off the cloisters on the opposite side from the path which led onto the herb garden. The doves lived in this beautiful little oasis within the main Abbaye grounds. The young monk fed them daily and this was why he crossed the courtyard in this way. I could imagine him tending them and being so gentle and full of care that they would flock around him and feel safe in his presence. It seemed to me he was as I imagined Christ Himself to be, the purity of vision, of thought and of deed all in one. It did not seem wrong to think this way, for had not Christ Himself lived on earth and was not He a humble carpenter?

I longed to be able to go with him and to see the doves. It would be so wonderful to experience the freedom they had in this loveliest of gardens, being able to soar on high above us, as we went about our daily tasks. Perhaps I longed for the escape that would mean; to be taken from this our earthly existence into the light, space and weightiness of another sphere. To be a part of this with the soul I held so dear was the greatest thing I could ever wish for.

I was to experience this wish sooner than I would have believed. As the months progressed and autumn began to fade into winter, I was to meet the young monk one crisp and bright December morning. I was on my way as usual to spend the hours I spent every day with the lepers, when once again I ran into this young man. We both stopped in our tracks, as it had been some time since our paths had crossed. It was as if the cold outside made the warmth inside our hearts blossom and I could feel his emotions as he smiled at me. This time we stood together and shared words for some ten minutes, which was the longest time we had ever spent together

I learned that his name was Brother Daniel and that he was from the north, from a family who were educated and had much knowledge of the church and its ways. He had a way of knowing things that was so fresh and bright and so exciting. He saw things differently from all others I had ever spoken with and it was as if his knowledge of life was far above many of the most learned people in the Abbaye. He was not puffed up with himself, but instead had a sense of humility which was stunning. His outlook on the sufferings of others was profound and I felt that in those ten short minutes I had learned more than I had learned from all my time in the Abbaye. I had a thirst to know all that he knew and I felt that this would be made available to me. We talked of life, of our beliefs in what life held and what we aspired to. He talked of his doves and of the joy and peace they gave him and he asked if I might wish to see the doves some day. My heart was so full of joy I knew not what to say, but he looked at me and said that he knew already the answer and my thoughts and that the time was close when he would show me the creatures he tended.

As it was close to the celebration of Christ's Mass, there was a lot of different activity in the Abbaye. I was to sing once again when we were all gathered for the celebration of the birth of Our Lord. Thus it was my daily routine was somewhat altered and I no longer visited the lepers at exactly the same times every day. It seemed there was a possibility that we could make an arrangement to meet clandestinely in order that I may visit the garden to look upon the doves. The day would dawn on the morning of the nineteenth day of December after matins and devotions. We were to meet at the well where he would wait for me.

Very early that morning I awoke with anticipation gnawing at my insides. I found for the first time that it was hard to concentrate in prayer and I had to focus properly and bring my attention to what I should have been doing. At last the time came for me to make my escape and this I did earlier than I would have normally done. It was lucky for me that I followed the pathway alone for no one noticed that I set off earlier than usual. As I crossed into the courtyard, I saw his habit by the well and my heart leaped with joy. It was a cold day, but not overcast and the light was beautiful as we made our way together in order not to draw attention to ourselves and it was with relief we passed through the gate and into the garden. The gate we passed through was not a particularly noticeable one in its shape and pattern and no one would have known what lay within. Even in the month of December I could appreciate how lovely the garden must be when in its prime. The quietude and serenity filled me with awe as I stepped forward to a small building in the middle of the garden.

As we drew closer, I could see hear the cooing of the doves inside and I saw one of them appear on the top of the vaulted roof. The birds were so beautiful and seemed to know that they were special to Brother Daniel. He went before me and spoke to them and gave them the food he was used to give them every day. They flew around him and above him and settled at his feet. I could not believe the beauty I saw before me. Then as if my joy was not enough he turned to me and said, "Look, Cecile, are they not as you and I? Do they not do as you and I would wish to – to soar above and to seek the freedom of the skies? They see in us the same needs they have themselves." He took my hands in his and held them out before him warming them from the winter chill. Then he lifted my hands to his lips and he kissed each finger so very, very gently and with such love the tears rose in my eyes and dropped on to the ground where the doves surrounded us.

Feelings freeze sometimes like drops of water in winter. The feelings that overtook me in that moment were to stay with me forever. No matter how much more involved we were to become and no matter how tangled our tale was to be woven, the memory of that moment when he first kissed my fingers is the one closest to my heart. I know that our love was heavenly, of the doves themselves, pure and unbesmirched and there for us to take. It was the reason we had been put on earth and it was so strong, nothing could keep us apart or away from accepting and feeling this emotion.

We were to meet many times in that beautiful sanctuary surrounded by the doves of hope. We both knew that we had crossed a threshold, which was not one we should have crossed, being in the situation we were in as nun and monk, but it was as if there was no turning back. Daniel was so knowledgeable about life and about hope and he taught me so much. I would sit at his feet in the garden, as he told me of things I had never heard of before; of our reasons for being born, for our belief in ourselves, in the knowledge that life would unfold as we made it and as it should unfold. He taught me about the flowers and the plants and their ability to heal. I knew, of course, a lot through having worked with the lepers in the hospital, but his knowledge was greater and as if he knew it from within and did not need to learn it from anyone else.

As the seasons passed and our lives became intermingled, I knew I should not talk of my love for Daniel with anyone else. If I told then it would seem somehow tarnished and I would feel guilt, which I did not feel now. I was, however, to entrust my secret with one person, as the circle of events unfolded.

We had made it possible to meet once every two weeks in the garden and had become wily in using ways to communicate with each other. We conversed by using the language of the flower and the plant and we had our own code by which we could decipher each other's messages. As the light came back into our lives and the winter darkness rolled away its cloak, to cast no more dark shadows on the days, it seemed to us that we could no longer feel safe together in the garden as we would both wish. Both Daniel and I longed for more time to spend in conversation and with each other.

Turning around the days and their duties caused this difficulty to be overcome. My work with the lepers in the Saint Lazare became curtailed for a short time, as I fell ill with an ailment, which caused me to become exceptionally tired. I could no longer cope with the long hours I spent with the lepers and I was not of such great use to them as I was usually. I suffered pain in my joints and my head was heavy and would not allow me to concentrate. I was advised by the Sisters to rest and to recover my strength, as I was now of great importance within the hospital. I had become very proficient in my treatment of the lepers, both in the practical aid and in the care of their souls. The Sisters of the hospital wished me to become well as quickly as I could and thus I was given time to recuperate and return to more work in prayer and thought.

At first this caused me great alarm as I knew that I could no longer meet Daniel in the same way, but then it fell upon me that it would help us to meet in some other way instead. I was prescribed fresh air and sunshine and was allowed to walk in the environs of the Abbaye during a certain period of the day. The Abbaye grounds stretched far afield towards the river in the one direction and in the other direction into the woods of the Foret de Fontevraud. I spent many hours exploring the areas around the great Abbaye and found much solace and happiness in the beauty of the countryside around me.

There were others who had tasks outside of the Abbaye and into the Abbaye grounds. One of those was my fellow sister and beloved friend, Columbine. She had, as one of her many tasks, the gathering of sticks, twigs and foliage in the forest to use for fires and to strew on the floors of the convent. It was a task she executed with joy as she, like me, loved the outdoors winter, summer, spring and autumn, for the possibility of catching Nature in her different shrouds. In spring it was so beautiful as Nature wore her dazzling coat of greens and lightsome yellows, which made all men want to rejoice and welcome the happiness back into their lives.

I accompanied Columbine on several occasions into the Foret de Fontevraud and on one of these occasions we happened upon Brother Daniel. He was gathering nuts from the forest and it was a great shock to me when we came upon him. I was so overjoyed to see him, but, of course, it was impossible for me to show my joy as Columbine would have known what was afoot. I struggled so hard to hold my emotions in check, but I could not allow for the fact that Daniel could not curb his. He saw only me to start with and called out my name for me to join him. It was then Columbine appeared from behind the trees where she had been gathering twigs. Her face told me all that I needed to know; she had understood at once the connection between the two of us, as nuns and monks did not address one another, even less use the proper name of the one in question.

In all my life I had never lied, not even once as a child, as my guilt would have shown directly in my face. It was never a difficulty for me to hide guilt for I was so innocent I concealed nothing from my family. Now I was confronted with guilt for the first time in my life. I knew that the feelings I had for Daniel were true and were meant to be. I was totally sure that not to love this man was the wrong thing for me to do. God had blessed us with the feelings we had and feelings cannot be changed or erased in the blinking of an eye. They cannot be erased at all until the feelings have died or changed in some other way. To try to eradicate a feeling, which is felt in the soul, is as pointless as tearing the clothes from one's body in winter in order to make yourself warm. The feeling of guilt, however, was also a feeling, which was new to me and almost hurt me as it gnawed inside my stomach. How could I lie to the one true friend I had and in whom I trusted completely? Thus I realized that I could not lie.

I knew that Columbine would not accept a lie from me: she was too sensitive to the way I was for this.

Daniel realised my plight then and told Columbine that it was not our wont to speak this way, but we had had occasion to meet while in the herb garden of the apothecary. It was a glossing over of the situation, but for the time it was enough to allow us to carry on our tasks and to take our leave. My heart was bursting with the need to speak to Daniel, but this time it could not be and I knew that I had to see him again and to be with him. I longed for his company and his being, as if the skin on my back was being burned by the sun and I needed shade and healing. He gave me the healing I needed in life and at this time, I knew he was the healing my mind so badly needed to help my body through its turmoil. His way of being and his love and compassion were all that my soul longed for.

My words to Columbine came with difficulty. I had no way around this problem other than to tell her the truth. The truth was that I loved this man more than any other human being; he was my waking thought, my comfort all day long, my final vision before I slept and even in sleep he was the bearer of tidings to me in dreams. He was, in essence, my very all, as though without him, I was no longer a whole being. It was with these emotions I had to live my life from this day on and if I loved this way then was it not right, for was not Jesus Christ, the Lord of Love? Was not love the most important thing to experience on this earth? My mind could not separate the love I had for Jesus and the love I had for Daniel. I loved them both with every fibre of my being and thus it could not be wrong to love this way. I was guided by Christ Himself and thus it must be right.

When friendship is truly felt, words are not necessary. No words can harm the heart if the feelings are true. If there is honesty, peace reigns in the heart, be it a hard lesson to learn or not. It is with honesty we show our truest and most beautiful love, for honesty is the trust, which dwells deep in our being. In being honest, using words, which may hurt or cause great pain is only done to uncover the true pain, which may be at root at the depths of the heart. When honesty is shared with joy the depths within soars high above the personage and welcomes the words. When honesty is shared in pain, the emotions soar even higher within the being that dwells within, for it opens up a knowing and a feeling of truth and recognition, which transforms the pain into acceptable pain and the ability to change and move forward in love.

Columbine proved herself to be that friend; the friend who is closest to one's heart and who will accept whatever is within without question. She knew in her head that what I was doing in my friendship with Daniel was very wrong, but in her heart, she knew it was the right thing for me to do, for my soul felt in a way that was so true and so filled with love it could not be wrong. It was not a matter that was to be discussed often between myself and Columbine . It was enough that we had been honest with each other and that there were no secrets. I knew that our friendship would not be put in jeopardy and neither would that of Daniel and myself.

Knowing that Daniel had been in the forest that day I took to walking in that area of the Foret de Fontevraud during the days that followed, in the hope that I may happen on him again. He had no doubt been of the same mind, for it was only a matter of days before we chanced upon each other yet again. This time we were both alone.

Daniel was collecting leaves and pieces of plants, which were to be taken to the Abbaye apothecary for use in the hospital. At this time of year, spring almost early summer, there was a great wealth in the cornucopia of nature's stocks. There were remedies available all around ready to be picked and used and thus there was much to be done in the woods and hedgerows at this time. When my mind was to wander in the months that lay far ahead, my thoughts very often came back to that early afternoon when we met in the forest. This time we were totally alone and needed not heed others who may hear us or find us in a place we should not have been. The forest was large and we could take care to find sufficient refuge where a passer by would not notice us. We were used to being secretive and thus this was no difficulty for us to overcome.

We found a sheltered spot in the forest, where there was soft moss and gentle undergrowth, where we could sit together with ease. Daniel was able to stay for some time as he had only just arrived before me and for once we did not feel that time was against us. It was so refreshing to hear his voice and to talk of the things we so needed to talk of. In him I found a soul who understood me completely and who could furnish my every wish in thought. That I was the same to him made my heart glad.

Being a child who had grown up with animals around me I was used to spring as a time of joy when the young of the beasts around us would be born. I knew all of the processes, which took place, in order that these little beings may be placed on earth by their mothers. It had, however, not occurred to me that man and woman should perform an act not unlike that of the animals. How could I know that what was to take place between man and woman as they came together was the ultimate sensation of ecstasy one would ever exist in. I was to discover this in that fresh and joyful afternoon, which made my life even closer to heaven.

It is from life on earth we see things happening around us. Behind us in our shaded spot we were surrounded by an oak tree, symbolic of strength. If we look on life on another plane we see the tree as the soul aspiring to the light and the tree also symbolises trust that we will reach the realms we aspire to on our journey. From a tiny acorn seed to a huge oak, the tree grows and is nurtured and learns and leaves its learning in its trunk and in its roots so that we may study it and know it as the being as it is, was and always has been.

In that afternoon Daniel and I were as two branches of the tree. I remember the moss we lay upon, soft as the thistledown in the quilts I lay under as a small child. Moss as soft as thistledown and your body as soft as down on my warm body as I held you and we became one. I remember the smells of the forest, the soft caress of your fingers on my face, your breath falling upon my lips as you bent forward and kissed me. We are as two parts of a puzzle; we are opposite and we are like. We are as two swans with necks entwined, we are as the eye and the needle, the bindweed around the vine. We are always two as one. I remember the moss soft as thistledown; I remember love; I remember you; I remember all that life is worth. I have it too and nurture it in this moment forever encapsulated in my memories.

Throughout the days and nights which followed,

my heart was so full of love it could not ever be empty again. The love I had experienced for and from another soul was the greatest and most beautiful experience I had ever had. If life was no longer to be lived I could progress into the heavenly spheres knowing that I had reached the ultimate goal I had come to experience. In meeting Daniel I had met the other part of my soul. The longing and the emptiness, which had been part of my life since a small child was no longer. Never had I acknowledged this feeling, but it had always been present. I longed for what was my right; to be with the soul who knew me better than any other; to merge with the beingness of that other soul and to experience total oneness as oneself, but also with another.

Love is the bud within us which transforms and allows us to grow in joy and creativity. It is the thought, which comes for the sake of another human being in peril; it is the solace of a mother for a child on its deathbed; it is the burgeoning joy of a heart that opens and wishes to fly away and to proclaim itself to all others. My love for Daniel is and was insurmountable, pure and unbesmirched. It is as a newly blossomed flower, where the petals are still wet from the first dew it experiences. That flower is still as this in its pure beauty.

Many times the flower has been trodden upon and even broken into small pieces in order that it should shatter, but that is not possible. It is still as sweet and as pure to me everyday of my life and every hour of my soul's turning. Never shall it be tarnished by what others would have me believe. If the love from the other soul was not the same does it matter, as I know the real soul within who knows me and has known me throughout eternity. No matter what and no matter how it changes or is put down, there will be no change in the emotion, which abides in the depths.

* * *

To be able to accept what is put upon us, we must have faith in God. My belief in that what I did, was for the truest and highest good of all, was always behind me. Could I have known what would transpire, it would not have shaken me from the feelings of certainty I had experienced. To be engulfed in feelings such as these was so overwhelming it was not possible to slough them off. Belief in an outcome that is positive is always the way ahead; to allow the negativity of one's thoughts to take over in fear is the least likely way to achieve the growth of the soul.

We were not to meet again in the woods during that early spring season. Daniel seemed to be engaged in other pursuits and I, myself, was put to other tasks, which did not tire me as much as the work in the hospital. It cheered me to be able to collect my thoughts in other ways, for I was so lost in my feelings of love it was hard to be in the moment. The ecstasy I had experienced with Daniel was of the starry spheres and far beyond what I have ever believed could be true upon this earth.

Columbine was wont to be with me when I spent time in the Abbaye gardens and thus we had an opportunity to speak of what was within my mind. Her fear when I uttered to her my feelings for Daniel and the love we had experienced was obvious immediately upon her face. It was sheer terror that lit inside her eyes; terror for the future and what was to be. I will never forget the words, which passed across her lips. "Cecile, you know what you have done! You have committed a deadly sin against God himself – you who are a Sister of Christ. This is to be the event of your downfall. How can you ever repair what has been done?"

The words were driven into my heart like heavy wooden nails and it was almost as if I felt the blood chilling in my veins. In my own world where truth and love reigned, the light of day in this earthly world had almost stopped reaching to my inner depths. Only now did I become afraid and filled with a feeling, which I supposed must be remorse. And yet I had no remorse. The love I had for Daniel was perfect and it was returned fully by him and I know Jesus Himself looked down on this bond as the greatest of the soul.

That moment when Columbine's words penetrated my ears, it seemed as if my life had suddenly stopped and been held up for all to see. "Look at her. See the harlot for whom she is. The Bride of Christ who besmirches His sacred name." I could hear the taunts before they were even uttered. Oh what a life it is at times when we succumb to our deepest feelings and pray for deliverance from on High. I prayed and prayed for help from Jesus, Mother Mary and God Himself to cleanse me from the sin I had committed, but never did I receive a chastisement from those Holy ones who heard my feverish prayers. The answer I was given was always that it was as it should be. How could there be such a difference in the beliefs of this world and that of the Higher Spheres? Why was I such an innocent in such matters? Why had I been created in this way? Was I some form of deviant from the norm?

There is great fear apparent when doubts are allowed to take hold. My body held this fear and transformed it into a form I had never felt before. My heart pounded and throbbed and sent messages to the rest of me to make all my limbs shake and be out of control. It took the depths of belief within me to conquer this feeling of unrest. I prayed and prayed more and more to my beloved Jesus Christ to help me in this plight I, alone, had put myself in. It was as if the knowledge from my mind had cloaked my heart and hidden the depths of truth and belief in that all that had taken place was right and proper as looked on by those who loved me truly from above. My fear had cloaked the area of certainty and hidden it from the light of true love. I had now become only the mortal part of my being and that beautiful connection with my beloved Saviour had been taken away, but only by myself.

We wander these pathways so very alone, but it is our own belief that we are alone. We, ourselves, create the fear inside and cause ourselves to leave the path of certainty. We are never alone and it is this need to doubt ourselves, which cuts us off from our true source of nourishment, God Himself. It took many hours of contemplation and doubt, many hours of deep soul searching and many hours of self hatred, before I could once again connect with the deepest feeling of peace and tranquillity that was always there. I had called myself a sinner, judged myself and thus judged my God, for was not He the being who is all for all of us. Is not our connection with the source of all, God, our salvation and not our downfall? The trap of the human mind is great, like a net that one is caught in and held captured. What we do not see is the light that enters the net at all times. We are never in darkness. We only create the illusion of such, through our own fear, which holds us separate from the love, which is always there. Once the picture was clear, that I was always and will always be a being of Light, the path ahead was lighter and more easily trodden, despite the repercussions, which were to be heaped upon me in the days to follow.

* * *

The month of June was to be a turning point in my life. I remember the morning when my soul finally became lost again from the salvation of God

Himself. It was to be a fated day in all ways both in the manner of how it came about and also in the way events unfolded and propelled me onwards. I had dwelt greatly upon the love between Daniel and I over the days that had followed our tryst, but I had never set eyes on him again. I had been able to carry the feelings of love in my heart with me from dawn to dusk and at times in sleep as it felt at times that we visited each other while in the dream state. It was not an easy situation after some time, as it became plain that we were not to be given the same chance to meet as easily again. I had recovered from my illness and was once more at use among the lepers. Days went past, but never did I meet his gaze nor touch his hands again. I fell into an element of longing, which took over my whole being. I was wont to fall on my knees at times with nausea and aching in my body, an ache, which caused no pain, but which seemed to dredge away all the lifeblood within me. I fell to longing for the evening, when I could at last rest. I believed I once more had succumbed to a sickness and at length I sought the advice of Columbine.

The Sacred Heart

My fears of an outcome, which was going to engulf me and almost drown me were to be made real. I, who had always seen the sunshine in every situation, was now to be dealt a hand wherein I could see no light, no refuge, nor even any hope. I was overwhelmed with fear, but also consumed by longing. Love had touched me in another form; the form of heartache. Love is still with us in those moments; we alone allow the fear to swarm around us like a swarm of bees, making itself present all around us, within us and without us. The bees of fear are always present, until we deal with the swarm, which is by dealing with the queen bee, she who is at the root of the disturbance, she who represents our greatest fear.

I sought the companionship of Columbine to ask for her guidance on this strange malady in my body. As I told her of my symptoms her face became pale and she looked so afraid I was concerned for her own welfare. "Cecile," she gasped. "Do you not know what it is that ails you? Have you not thought of your closeness with this monk, whom you hold in such high esteem? What have you done?"

I looked at her, but could not see any answers forming in her face. There was only fear. "Columbine," I cried. "Please tell me what it is you know and I do not."

Her reply was to send my blood churning in my veins, as if someone had poured ice cold water from the frozen water barrel into me. I positively froze. The realisation that I was with child took over my whole being and I began to shake and wail. I could not control my emotions, despite knowing that others may hear me. I was no longer in control of myself in any way. Columbine was, as always, my human saviour. She held me and caused me to cease the fearful wailing, until it was only the racking sound of low sobs that could be heard. The sickness within me welled up at the same time and it was a relief to my system to let go, as if letting go of all the fears within me at the same time.

There is an awareness within us, which allows us

to move forward even when we are totally paralysed. It may not be a physical movement, but it is a movement either through the thoughts or the emotions. My emotions at this time were not to be relied upon and thus I was left to rely upon my logic and the thoughts, which swayed around in my head, like a boat without a destination on a stormy sea. I had to be the skipper, the man at the helm and the sea of emotions were to be controlled and put in their place. There had to be a destination no matter what the challenge inside. The fear became less than the need to move and thus the logical side of me took control and moved into a place of conscious denial.

What was was, what had been had been and now the situation was to be accepted. God had always sent mercy in all situations. Why would this situation be any different? I became the master of my fate and in so doing pretended in myself that the situation would come right in the end. I would be led to a place of solution, solace and forward movement. God was my all and my provider and he would provide for me, aid me and sustain me through this challenge too.

I informed Columbine that God and my beloved Jesus Christ would watch over me and bring me a solution in this dilemma. She was not to refer to my condition nor to treat me with any difference. I would be the one who would ask for help if I saw this as being necessary. Now I see how flawed my view of my situation was and I feel sad and sometimes resentful with myself for being so naïve, but how could I react otherwise. What other course of action was there for me than the one that I had never even considered. Life is life no matter what. We are given life, we sustain it until such time as the flame goes out. We do not consider that we have the right to extinguish a flame ourselves.

By my lack of consideration of the situation, due to my naivety and denial, I was to bring myself into a trap. I, alone, was the maker of my fate. I did not envisage that someone would become aware of my physical condition hidden under a habit as I was, but the physical symptoms, which plagued me were to come to the attention of one of the older nuns. She often dealt with those of high birth, who found their way to the Abbaye, due to a similar situation to my own. These young ladies would be sheltered by the Abbaye until such time as the fruit of their womb was delivered and taken care of and then set free to resume their destiny albeit not unscathed.

The nun, of whom I speak, cared for these young ladies and was well acquainted with the symptoms a woman with child experiences. She noticed in me the symptoms she dealt with on a daily basis and thus my subterfuge was no longer able to carry on. I had been exceptionally sick one morning and despite having tried to hide this, I had to run from my duties. Sister Maria Teresa followed me and enquired after my health and my continued need to let go of the contents of my stomach. "How long have you felt this way?" she asked, with a look, which made me shiver with fear. I knew there was no good in lying to her and I told her that I had been in this condition for quite some time. The sigh which followed and the look upon her face confirmed inside me that my greatest fear was now at my door.

Sister Maria Teresa was a kind soul, despite her diligence to duty and her need to conform to the rigid disciplines of convent life. She calmed me by saying that it would be best for me to speak to the Mother Superior about the plight, which had befallen me. Her sense of shock was great and it was as if there were no words she could communicate to me to change the situation either for good or for bad. The shock and the shame were too great for her to handle. Perhaps it may have seemed that some miracle had occurred, which could hide me from this most uncomfortable and hideous situation.

My debt to Mother Superior became so great within my heart, that I could not let the thoughts of it lie at any time of the day. That this woman was a saint in an earthly shape I have no words to deny. I looked to her for my salvation, but also for my succour and she dealt me both with great love. To admonish me would have been of no use, as the deed was done and the only thing that I could do to save myself from her sadness was to tell her how deeply I had loved this man. I could not, however, disclose his personage and it was this that caused me great turbulence in my soul. The need to protect Daniel was greater than the need to protect myself. The thought for my unborn child was not even apparent; so naïve was I. It was as if I carried a kitten or small bird in my bloomingness and not a human child, who one day would be just as I. What lack of thought, what innocence and what folly!

Heaven helps us when we call and in so many ways. When we are in debt to our creator for our very being on earth, at the one time we see the patterns of our earthly knowledge become so easily tied up and misshapen. In this period of my life all was as if a ball of twine had been pulled and torn at by mad cats in a brawl. My life had no real purpose left other than to survive each day away from the knowledge of the others, that I had strayed from Christ's flock and was at once a lost and hapless sheep.

This period of sadness and despair was to escalate in the months ahead, but it was as if through this desolation I gained a strength I had never known before. I was able to cope with the feelings of sorrow and even of failure as if by magic. I gained a sense of belief that had never touched me before. I became as one with my creator, instead of as one shunned by her creator. Each day seemed to me to be filled with praise despite fears of what may happen in the days to come. It was as if someone had given me the power to forget what might be and instead to dwell on what was. Perhaps there was a purpose in all that was taking place; a greater purpose for others to understand and to look upon. It was as if my fate was an important one, although fearful, and had to happen in order for others to know of it. None of this, of course, made sense in a logical way, but to the workings of the soul it was crystal clear. This situation had come about to aid and to teach, no more and no less.

There are moments in life when you reach inwards for help, as there seems to be no outward posts to hold on to. These last months of my growing child were to be of this kind. I had remained within the Abbaye practically unseen by all others due to the care of the Mother Abbess herself. I had been put under the surveillance of Sister Maria Theresa and was treated as one of the higher orders in the same way that their predicament was hidden from the eye of the common observer. I was able to live like this, as I spent most of my time in prayer as well as doing menial duties, which I could still carry out without being a part of a greater community. My closeness to the outer world was much less than before and I longed for my walks in the forest. I would have loved to hear the wind sighing in the trees, the sound of birdsong and the soft lapping of water as it reached the bank. My memories of that wonderful time were locked in my heart and I was almost afraid to think of Daniel lest I was overcome with too deep an emotion. That I longed for him and thought of him, that I cannot deny, but I refused to myself the joy of remembrance. My body ached with every fibre of my being to see him and to look upon that beloved face once again, but I denied myself the pleasure of remembering the moments together.

The heartache, which arose from the cessation of the union, which was at once divine and of this world was indescribable. Our union had created a life, a life that I was never to see growing and becoming an adult. I was to be rid of this flame and the source of our love as if it were a taper stamped upon and made to go out. I tried not to think of this ache within me and instead dwelt upon what was before me at any given time. It was not for me to suppose what would happen. That was in the hands of the Divine Himself as He saw fit to allow. I had secured the body I lived in, but the life that was to be was not completely my concern. I could influence its passage, but only to some extent. The pathway was already mapped out albeit in a loose fashion, but still mapped out. It was not for me to cry out for change, for this I know was my destiny, my reason for being, but also my downfall.

* * *

There are many times in life when we reach for others to save us in our deepest despair.. The one whom I called my dearest friend was to be this person - Columbine. At first she had held herself apart from me as if the role she played was too complicated. Her words of shock at the first instance of knowing my plight had caused her to withdraw, thinking I felt she no longer cared about me. This of course could never be the case, but she feared this nonetheless. It took some time and words of comfort from the Mother Abbess herself, to lead her back to my side. She came to me with a touch of fear in her eyes. Fear that I would turn her away, but if she thought this, she could not have been more wrong. The love I felt for her was too great ever to be tarnished and thus we found each other again. She was the rock I leaned upon in the stormy sea of life. Her own fears were now hidden as she nurtured me and consoled me and gave me the love I so desperately needed. It was accepted by the Mother Abbess as well needed, in this most desolate of situations. I wonder even now that I was not admonished nor caused humiliation, but such was the greatness of the Mother Abbess. She was to me as the vision of Mother Mary Herself.

From a state of acceptance, I was to fall once more into the depths of new emotion. This time an obsession that I knew I could not placate without actually facing my beloved. I loved him from the depths of my being, but my love was tainted by my sudden lack of belief in that he loved me in the same way. I knew in my heart that he did so, but my heart grew heavier and heavier with doubt, until one day Columbine decided that enough was enough and that something had to be done to alleviate my distress. She feared for my sanity and for the health of the unborn child and decided to make it her duty to seek out Brother Daniel and to face him with the truth.

This decision had not come to her with ease and she was unsure as to how this meeting should come about, but she was aware of the meeting places we had had and made it her mission to seek out Brother Daniel in the herb gardens of the apothecary. As it was now summer the doves did not need to be fed, as in winter, and Daniel would not have his errands there. This was, in essence, a dangerous mission, as any contact between nun and monk was shunned. This we had known, but fate had dealt us fortune in that we had been able to cause this to happen. Columbine had more difficulty in this, as she did not attend to the herbs of the garden as I had. Luck was to be on her side despite all, as she came upon Daniel briefly on an occasion near the cloisters. She was hurrying along on an errand and saw him in the distance, his tall figure and gait obvious even from afar. She slipped along as deftly as she could in order to gain on him and was able to make a very short contact as she passed by. Her words were only, "Cecile - meet by dovecot." She did not have the possibility to say when this should come about and thus gave herself the task of being there as often as was possible. I helped her in this by using the language of the flowers we had built up together and thus it was she came to tell him of my fate.

The man, Daniel, was as though two people in one being. The beloved, the man of spirit and of the cloth was the one I had come to know and to trust, as well as to love from the depths of my soul. That there was another side to this person I had never contemplated, but I was to find this out in the most painful way. The time had come for me to learn that Daniel was not the man I had dreamed he was and it was to shock me so much that my heart almost stopped beating within my breast. I found out from Columbine that she had made contact with Daniel after many lost opportunities over the last weeks. She had, however, made his acquaintance on a day when the sun shone and the clouds had rolled away over the heavens. I was so sure in my heart that he would be so sad and thoughtful for my plight, the words Columbine brought back to me were to cause me the greatest pain I would ever endure. Even in the times ahead, whatever befell me could not hurt me more than the words I heard repeated from Columbine. "I have never lain with a woman. Cecile is lying to herself. I can not be the father of her child. I have never in my life known a woman. She lies and blames me to protect herself in her plight. I thought better of her than this. It was my greatest fault to befriend a nun in the first place. Folly, folly, folly. Tell her our acquaintance must be over for good!"

* * *

Madness is the word to describe how my thoughts formed and propelled me into behaving. Madness, complete and full. Madness. That is all that can be said to describe my behaviour and my thought processes over the following days. Talking to myself, wringing my hands in torture of the spirit, casting myself on the depths of darkness within myself. Where was my faith now? Where was my God, my beloved, my dearest heart, the Lord Jesus, my Saviour? I felt that there was no one, no being whether in this world or in another who could help me, understand me or save me. I had reached the edge where desperation lies and was almost beyond the pale. I now understood how the human soul can shut down and run from its own sanctuary. When the soul loses its footing in its human body and no longer has the strong foothold on the beauty and wonder of the divine, it casts itself upon the very darkness we come here to enlighten. Only then when it is darkest do we start to see the glimmer of light, which is at the end of the tunnel. That glimmering, shimmering light that refuses to be put out.

It was for my greatest good that fate delivered me into the hands of my beloved Mother Abbess. She was aware of the great sin I had committed, but also knew me as an innocent, who had no real grasp of everyday life as it was outside the Abbaye. I was protected by her as she saw the deep connection I had with my beloved Jesus Christ and the way I was able to be totally at one in my devotion and my access to the secrets, which lay behind that deeply spiritual connection. Had she not been the woman she was, she may have called me a heretic, as my path seemed so different to others, but never did she contemplate this. She, herself, was a woman who walked a wider and more profound path in the world of men and male dominance. She was aware of her need to conform to the path she was called to walk at all times, but also deeply aware of her commitment to her Sisters and fellow nuns, whose fate she often held in her hands. Not for her was the path of servility under the auspices of men; she had been given a special place and a special role to hold the divine spirit of womanhood alive in a world almost totally ruled by the ways of men. That she was in a religious order of women, who were the Brides of Christ, helped to hide the power that she held in her hands. Had she been in any other position her authority would have been taken from her very swiftly.

My life was to change from this day on. The recognition of what could be was vast. A nun, a Bride of Christ, complete and virginal – how could she be taken by a man? What man would do such a thing? The only men who were in the vicinity were the monks. Never could it be conceived that a monk could carry out something so base. If the Mother Abbess considered otherwise she would not allow it to be known. Her thoughts must have been above all to shelter me and to shelter the reputation and safe space, which the Abbaye was. Her decision to protect me in this fate was final. Her love for me proved to be much greater than I was ever able to understand and as I look back on the past and the way events were played out, I realise how much she gave up of her own reputation and safety in order to save me. "Greater love hath no man than this, that a man lay down his life for his friends." The Mother Abbess was willing to do this for me and once again I learned the lesson of love in its purest form; the lesson of unconditional love, which accepts, forgives, nurtures and only sees the soul as perfect.

* * *

The soul craves the balance between the feminine and the masculine. It may take longer to accept one aspect over the other and thus we are drawn back time and time again until we bring into equilibrium the parts of each gender we fight against and deny. This pattern repeats itself over and over until we are truly balanced and ready to transcend this our life on earth as a soul. Many lifetimes are spent in this learning and the power struggle between man and woman and which is the most powerful, is one which will continue until such time there is a balance and understanding at exactly the same point between the male and the female gender.

The Mother Abbess was a woman of high virtue and integrity. She was able to devise ways of allowing balance to be resolved in situations where others would have walked away or lost the ability to see both sides of the equation. She had an understanding of the needs of each person she dealt with, whether they appeared as kind and willing souls or as souls whose dark side was the more apparent. She judged not, but weighed each person's rights in her mind in such a fair way that it was almost impossible for those with a darker motive to take command. Such was her sense of justice and by way of her kind and loving attitude she was able to waylay any threats, which may have caused her consternation. This did not, however, mean that she was unable to stand firm and to be strong if faced by those who did have the tendency to push her to a certain limit. She had power and a great sense of self, which held her fast and strong in all she undertook.

The Mother Abbess had been pushed to answer questions concerning me. Words had been exchanged to do with my predicament. Although it had been kept as quiet as possible the knowledge of my situation had seeped out. Even in the Holiest of orders, there is a certain gossip and need to share the failings of others. I was never to learn who the source of this was and it is really of no importance other than that it caused great problems for me. The news was to be bandied around among the churchmen who looked for reasons to usurp the Mother Abbess at each turn. Even at this point she protected me and held me in the safety of her loving kindness. She was, however, pushed to the limits, allowed to give me the time for my child to be born, but once this was over I would be put to the test to give the identity of the man who had used me. I knew that Daniel's name would never cross my lips no matter what might befall me and the Mother Abbess knew this too. I have never fully understood her acceptance of my situation, but I take it to be the love for her fellow human being and the knowledge that she, herself, could have found herself in a similar situation given different circumstances.

That I was afraid of what lay ahead of me was the absolute truth no matter how I tried to hide it from myself. What was to happen during the actual act of giving life to another human being was one enormous part of the fear inside me. How would it feel? Would it be painful? Would I survive the actual birth? What would happen to me after this child was born?

Many times I reminded myself of the huge amounts of love I had experienced in my life, at times when there was no one there to give it to me. The love came from some place within me, which was endless and always there. It was the simplest thing to access this love, purely by connecting my thoughts to that place in my heart and it would fill me with the purity of the greatest love there ever was. Now I connected to this place and spent many hours in a space of meditative silence, which even transcended the power of prayer. It was a place of ease, calm, peace and total acceptance. A place where I felt accepted, never judged and always supported. With hindsight, and the ability to transcend time, I can now see that I was in a heavenly place, where we all connect at some point. That I was able to take solace from this place even in times of great fear was truly amazing.

During my confinement I was tended by my true

and loving friend, Columbine. She treated me like a delicate flower, which was to be nurtured and given all that was needed to grow and blossom. The hours spent with Columbine are those I cherish most. We did not talk much due to the devotions we had to follow, but there was never any real need to do so. We knew within our hearts that our time together could be curtailed at any time. The presence of another loving soul was of such comfort to me that I can never express it in terms of value. I was deeply grateful to the Mother Abbess for the time we were given together.

There was to come a day, however, when I knew that a change was to come. As my belly grew and the child within kept me awake in the hours of darkness as I struggled to lie in a comfortable position, I knew that my time of waiting would soon be over. I did not dare to connect too closely with this soul within me who would some day soon walk this earth. I was afraid that I would not be able to cope with the loss of this little person, who I would not be able to love and cherish as the fruit of my womb. I had no idea what would happen after this child was born, but I knew that there was no possibility of my being the mother the child so desperately needed. I knew I had brought shame on myself, but also on the Abbaye and I knew that the Mother Abbess had given me the greatest gift in allowing me to stay on and to be nurtured during this growing time. There was no earthly way possible to stay on in the Abbaye as a nun with a child. I knew that my future, no matter how it was to unfold, did not contain this wondrous child I held in my womb. There were times when I allowed my thoughts to drift to how the child would appear once born. Would he/she resemble me or would she have the blue eyes that lit up my heart whenever I allowed my thoughts to stray to the memories of Daniel? Each time my thoughts strayed I had to bring myself back to he reality that was now.

The feelings of love for this man, who was the other half of me, were so great I could forgive him anything. I could forgive him the need to run away and to hide from the shame we had brought on ourselves. What is shame in essence? Shame is the stigma placed on you by others who do not understand your thinking or your actions, as they do not feel nor see the experience. Shame is felt in the words of someone who sees only their way of perceiving; shame is in the eye of the beholder who views only one part of the enactment of the whole play that is our life; shame is the shower of anguish and self loathing heaped upon oneself when dealt the words and views of others. Shame is the heaviest burden to carry, for it is not real, but we make it a reality. There is no shame in Heaven, for there are no wrongdoings or wrong choices. Shame and blame lead to loss, revenge and ultimately to the death of the soul. How can the beauty of the soul hold itself high when viewed as tarnished, torn and worthless? The answer is through love: love for oneself no matter what, love for oneself firstly and in loving oneself, loving the other from an understanding that they do not see the greater picture which is evolving. Love is the magic, which dissolves shame.

As the sunlight turned brighter and brighter and the newborn day showed itself from beneath its cloak of darkness, I awoke to the sense of tugging in my belly. It was as if there were ten men pulling at my insides, in order that they would be pulled out of me. I had begun to experience this in short spells over the last week or so and I was aware that this had something to do with the process of my child arriving on this earth.

As the sensations turned from purely acceptable to painful, I began to grow restless and called out as the sensation hit me once again and again. I was being tended in an area of the Abbaye, where there were other young women in a predicament similar to my own. I was, however, not to mingle with them and share their experiences, as even a deflowered lady of high birth who had been shamed, was on a much lesser level of depravity than a Sister of Jesus who had sinned in the same way.

It was with great relief that I heard the door opening and saw the face of Columbine peeping round.

"Cecile," she cried. "Is it your time?"

I was not able to reply, as a great surge of pain overcame me and pushed me on to my knees.

"Wait," she gasped. "I will fetch Sister Theresa and she will inform the Mother Abbess. Breathe my dearest one, breathe and think of your loving Jesus who is always with you. This pain is a positive pain, for it brings joy with it. Remember no matter what, you have created a new life, a soul to walk this earth, who will learn and grow no matter what the circumstances. You have always done what was asked of you. This soul knows this. Please remember this always. Your challenge has been to carry on in the knowing that this little one must be born. Breathe, breathe and pray?"

In a flurry she was gone and I was left panting and struggling. I had heard the screams of the other young women around me, but nothing had prepared me for the pain I was now feeling. It was as if through a mist I saw the chapter of events happen. Columbine returned with two of the sisters, who helped me to kneel and to push. Their expressions told me that there was some kind of trouble around the actual birthing and I searched their faces for the answer. Columbine was with me no matter what I was to encounter. She wiped the sweat from my forehead and gently held my hand and whispered soft encouragement into my ear, wiping the tears that flowed from my eyes.

At some point I became aware of the presence of the Mother Abbess and the whispers of the sisters around me. "Stuck – the wrong way to present" "Mother Mary pray for this soul." "Hurry and fetch

Sister Magdalene. She knows what to do."

Among the whispers I also heard the sound of men's voices. Men in the sacred inner space of a nunnery? Could this be true? Something was so wrong, so incredibly wrong, but the pain that swamped me was too great and too consuming for me to be able to take notice of what was happening around me.

Later I was to learn that the voices of the men were those of a higher power in the Abbaye, who took their following from the Mother Abbess, but who saw it as their political chance to usurp the power of the woman who led us all. Times were changing and the acceptance that a woman could be in charge was beginning to fade. This situation, which I had alone got myself into, was to cause a furore so great as to reverberate much, much farther than the safe confines of the Abbaye walls.

At some point the pain became so intense I must have passed out and when I awakened I saw the face of a man, who stared at me with such contempt. He was being pushed out of the door by the sisters, but his face is ever etched on my inner eye. The scorn and loathing he showed froze my soul, but even worse was the sight of lust beneath the scorn. This I will never forget! I who had had the purity of a newborn lamb, was now the booty of any man who followed the feelings caused at the sight of a woman. Where would my life lead to now? "A whore and harlot!" were the words I heard called out in the recesses beyond the room I had been taken to. Words that once again drove nails of shame and agony into my heart. I knew from the fracas outside that I was no longer the property of the Sisters and of the Mother Abbess. I was now the property of the world of men to have me and to use me whenever they wished. I had no fine house nor high birth to return to; I had reached the depths of the depths and life would never be the same. My fate was sealed.

When one reaches the true depths of the soul there is a turning point. That point is where we recognize our true nature and our connection to the greater part of existence. We are no longer what we think we are; we are so much greater. We reach the full stretches of our potential and we grow and thrive in our inner knowledge that life on this earth is one tiny, tiny spot in the time we inherit in the world of the universe and the spheres; the world of God, the creator of whom we are a part. Reaching this place was to allow me to let go: to let go of the agony of childbirth; to let go of my mortal shame; to let go of my fears for my child; to let go of my fears of loving Daniel as I did. As I let go within and I became peaceful and safe, so did my body let go and a rush came about within me as at last the child burst into this world to be caught in the arms of Sister Magdalene. What better name could a nun have to receive a child like this. The Magdalene, the whore who was not a whore, but a loving, living divine being of pure light. My child, my girl child would carry that name as a reminder that there is no such thing as debasement to do with the pleasures of the senses if lived through love; there is no debasement in that one is born into this world as a woman. My child, *my daughter*, would not suffer my fate. She would always know that she was conceived in love and truly loved by her mother, even if her father may not even know of her birth. Within her heart she would know that she was conceived of love.

I felt the arms of one of the sisters pull me up, out of my thoughts, as she placed this beautiful child into my arms. My daughter, my love, the union of two souls. I saw in her eyes the knowledge she carried, the connection to the depths of all that is and I saw it all in these blue eyes, those eyes, which could only be formed from the father whose name is Daniel. I knew then that we had succeeded in bringing each other into this new life. What her characteristics were to be and to develop into was not yet known, but that she had inherited her father's eyes and the shape of my face was already obvious.

The profundity of the love I felt for this small bundle was beyond words. I wanted to hold her and to love her and to keep her safe from anything, which could cause her harm in this life. I saw, too, that in her perfection she was deeply flawed. In the space where her mouth ought to have resembled a sweet cherry, there was a gaping hole, which made her in some way contorted and vulnerable. To my eyes she was still as perfect as she could ever be. That she had survived and been given life and breath was good enough. Perfection is only a human value that we must strive not to demand in outer ways. We, as souls, are always perfect and no matter what outer packaging we are born with, the soul inside shines like a living star. Even if my daughter was not perfect in the sight of others I knew, that in the eyes of God, she was as whole and as beautiful as she ever could be.

I knew from the faces of the sisters gathered around me, that there was fear in their hearts. They did not want to say anything for the moment, knowing that our time as mother and child was very limited. Despite their fears they wished to preserve this special bond, this outreach towards God in the breath of a new soul. There would be time to discus and ponder the other aspects of the child's birth at a later time.

At once I heard the voice of my saviour, the Mother Abbess. I call her my saviour not to blaspheme, knowing that my Saviour, Jesus Christ, holds us both in His hands. She was my earthly saviour, who was led by the guidance of Jesus and God Himself. Her voice was calm, although measured, as if there were words that were being held back by a floodgate, which must not unleash. Her concern for my welfare was, as always, the most important thing. As she looked down on my child, my Magdalene, my Madeleine, she smiled and took my hand.

"Cecile," she whispered. " No matter what is said or done from this moment forth know that God and our Saviour, Jesus Christ, blesses this child and confers upon her grace. To you he confers the knowledge that love in all its forms begets even more love. Remember this, my child. You will need it. As for the problem in the child's make up, this we see as a sign that we are not always perfect in our ways on earth and that the Creator deals us difficulties in which we can learn to grow and understand acceptance. You must be strong now as the time ahead will bring adversity and a true need to hold your faith strong. You must carry the knowledge of my..."

Her words were stopped by the door crashing open and the face of the man I had seen while in the throes of childbirth, launching himself into the small room where I lay.

"Here she is, the harlot, the perpetrator of sin within this holy place, this devil, this filth. Show me the fruit of the womb now!"

His harsh words and the sense of disgust, which tainted the sacred space he now defiled, changed everything.

"Show me the brat now!", he mocked and on leaning towards us his face recoiled in a sense of fear and revulsion. He crossed himself as he spat out the words "God in Heaven, behold the spawn of the devil! Look at this being. She," he roared, pointing at me, " has been in the hands of the Devil himself. No other creature can be conceived like this. She must be thrown out of this holy place or she will defile us all!"

He turned to the Mother Abbess and shouted "And you will know the consequences of your actions towards this depravity!" He turned on his heel and looking back over his shoulder he said with a look of revenge on his face, "You cannot hide her, I will be back and very soon with men to take her from this place. She is a contagion that could cause the downfall of the Abbaye. Be ready!"

The shock left in the room on his departure was tangible and was felt like waves crashing on a shore and destroying all in their wake. The sisters huddled together not knowing what was to be done. Our order was not a wholly silent one, but there were large areas of time where words were not used. This was to be a blessing in the situation we now found ourselves in. We were used to holding our thoughts within us and communicating when the time was appropriate. This helped us to focus and was advantageous in times of upheaval. Together we moved as one in testing situations. This was one of these situations and the power of the silence helped.

The Mother Abbess did as she always did and held the spirit of the Divine in the moment. With a new sense of direction she cautioned the sisters to hold their voices and thoughts to themselves and to follow her orders. She asked one of the sisters to take my child at once to the safest place she could; to the confines of the nunnery, where the nuns worshipped. Nobody could enter this space without her permission. She knew, however, that she may not do the same for me, as the consequences for all of her charges would be too great and this was as far as she could help me in my plight. I knew she would have offered her life for me, but she also knew that this time she could not. This was not just the case of a nun having succumbed to carnal knowledge, it was much deeper than this. My plight was to break forth the needs for the masculine presence within the Abbaye to seek the power and the authority it so greatly desired. Mine was not just a case of having done wrong through the church's doctrine; it was an opportunity for the men of the church to take charge and to push down the gentler understandings of the feminine way. The Mother Abbess looked deeply into my eyes and I saw her plight and her sorrow. "Cecile," she pleaded. "Tell me who the father is. You must tell me. This could mean your life. You must tell me. I beseech you!"

In my heart I knew I must answer her. I must tell her of my love for Daniel, for the beauty of our union and the equality of our souls in conceiving this child, but I could not. I had made a promise, a promise to someone whom I loved more than life itself. I could never, would never give his name. I knew not then that this was my challenge, my challenge to speak for myself, to speak for my existence, for the existence of my child. I knew only what my whole being was telling me, as I thought then, rightly, that it was my duty to withhold the name of Father Daniel.

Is love this wrong? Do we understand how we think or feel when love is involved at its deepest place? Wherein do we colour our judgements? How do we define our own needs with regard to the needs of another? Perhaps looking back I could have listened more to the words of my Saviour, "Love Thy neighbour as Thyself". Life is all a challenge to and a chance to advance the soul. Each lesson pushes us forward on our pathway, which leads us closer and closer to the Divine. In following this path I made choices, which would hold with me for a long time and for the space of many lifetimes. The Divine does not judge us, it only sees how we progress on a pathway. We are not admonished nor encouraged. We are simply observed and loved. Should we make a decision that could be detrimental, our guardian angels can but observe and help us as well as they can. They do not either judge, for this is not their challenge. They simply love us and make our pathways as smooth as possible in each individual circumstance.. They know that what we do not learn in one life we will learn again in another or another. For some souls, progression is quick and easily learned by the lessons chosen. For others the lessons can be held for many wanderings on this earth. We forget, however, that there are many lessons to be learned in each and every life and we learn more easily depending on the lessons. I know that I learned what love is, the love between a man and a woman and I know I learned it well; I learned what it is to give life and to lose this connection, but in doing so I learned that I could never erase that love and it dwelt with me always. I learned that I was a clear channel for many of my perceptions and that I was not afraid to confess to this knowledge brought from the spheres by the Divine. I was strong and I was proud to be a vessel used in this way.

In the end I chose another above myself and this was to be my challenge. It was, however, not for me to judge the other's behaviour. At this point it was enough for me to know that I loved Daniel and I would not regret that love, which was so pure and innocent, not for anything in this world. I already knew that my child would be taken away from me and this I had had time to prepare for. It would never have been my choice, but I was unable to follow the path I wished for, to be a mother and to nurture and care for a child. I was a nun, a failed one, yes, but still a nun. I knew that my daughter would be cared for. I knew it in my heart and this gave me solace.. I knew that the Mother Abbess would do all that she could to protect this life. She had seen an infliction similar to Madeleine's several times, when the daughters of high station gave birth. She knew it was similar to a humpback or a club foot. A sign of an imperfect body, but not an imperfect soul. I had to trust that she would find a way to save my child. For myself I asked nothing. I had sinned against the Holy Word and it was my punishment to take however it was meted out. As a soul on a path beyond the earthly I know now that I was wrong to believe this. I had never done anything but love and love can never be a sin.

Now came the moment I had dreaded; the moment when my child was taken from my arms. It is always possible to prepare oneself for a situation like this when it is not a reality. The anguish and the tearing away of part of my soul was something very different. I had held this small bundle, flawed yet so perfect, in my arms, for such a short time and it was the only time I would ever have with her. To give her away already was inhuman and yet I had to. I knew that her life depended on my ability to let go. I would know in my heart that she was cared for, as I knew the Mother Abbess would find a way for her to be looked after. I knew this as a truth. I had signed my daughter's fate the moment my eyes alit on Daniel.

Anguish and deep bottomless sorrow consumed me as I heard the cries of the child as she was passed from one nun to the other and then she was gone, the door closing tightly behind her. There I was now, alone, to serve my sentence. Alone on this earth without the two beings whom I loved so very much: Daniel and now, Madeleine.

I was to realise that I was not completely alone, as at that moment the sun burst through the clouds of my heart and I saw a light, a light that I had never seen before. I knew that I was a part of that light and that I was always safe. I was loved and I was cherished. I was an important part of the light and not some pathetic, helpless being. I had the strength of that light within me and it was always there, not just at this moment. The strength of this moment helped me to move both physically and spiritually. I was to carry this vision within me for ever after and it was this light, which held me in its arms throughout those dark and demonic times ahead.

The Mother Abbess reappeared in the room and this time I knew that she feared not only for my safety and for the safety of all her charges, but also for herself. She had been put in a situation, which had never arisen before. She had to think and act as clearly as she could to save us all. She ushered me to sit and she gave me fresh clothing and food. To eat at a time of day when food was not expected was alien to me after so long in the Abbaye. "Eat, child," she urged me. "You do not know when you will eat again."

I could barely swallow what was put in front of me, as the exhaustion of giving birth was still hanging heavily upon me, but I knew that I would need physical strength as well as the strength I had within me from the Divine.

"I do not know what will happen now," she said sadly. "But I will do everything within my power to help you. I know your sadness to do with the child and you must know that I will do my utmost to provide for her. She is safe for the time being. I will not reveal where she has been taken. I still hold power in this instance. Sadly I cannot protect you any longer, although my prayers and the prayers of the sisters will always be with you. I know that this has happened through innocence and I respect that, despite your actions going against the will of God. As a nun you have promised to be a bride of Christ and this cannot be broken, at least not with ease. You are still a nun in your heart and in the eyes of God, but in the eyes of the Church you are a lost soul. Please keep your faith strong in God, my child. This alone will save you. You cannot save whoever it is who has wronged you, as in the eyes of the Lord his punishment will be shame, shame within his heart for what he has done to you. Shame, not from God, but for his weakness and lack of compassion."

As I struggled to stand up, I was aware of how little strength I possessed. How was my life to be from now on? Where would I go or more likely, where would I be taken? I knew my fate lay in the hands of the man who would be back at any time to take me away as the evil being who could cause even more evil to spread within the Abbaye. My heart sank at the understanding of what this could mean.

I was not to wait much longer to discover where my path was to go, as the door once more crashed open and the voices of nuns trying to restrain the men in the corridor could be heard. Four men rushed at me, led by the man who I will now refer to as "the perpetrator of evil". I saw in him what he believed he saw in me. I was grabbed and thrust off the bed I lay on, causing me to fall onto my knees. One of the men took this opportunity to kick me from behind and I knew then that I was now of less worth than an animal.

The Mother Abbess and the sisters tried to help me up, but were pushed back and cautioned by "the perpetrator of evil". "Do not touch this instrument of the devil," he growled. "You can be contaminated. Where is the brat? What have you done with it?"

"The child has been taken," answered the Mother Abbess. "I abhor the treatment you mete out to this one of my sisters, but I will *not* accept this treatment towards a newborn child. This is not the way of a loving God and I will withstand any forceful measures you attempt to take. I am still the one who holds the power in the running of this Abbaye and you know that! Your belief in a devilish plot is a false one and you will live to regret what you do. This woman you see before you is but a child herself, despite being a sister of the Abbaye. She has had no involvement with anything devilish. If there is anything to do with the Devil here it is your conduct! You have no right to force yourself in here in this sanctuary of a nunnery. It is my place to mete out any punishment at this point."

The face of the man, whom I had begun to fear and loathe pushed itself closer to the Mother Abbess and he snarled at her, "Do not think that you are in command when this has happened in the Abbaye. She," he spat out in my face, "will be dealt with in the ways of the world, as she has succumbed her right to the protection of the this place. Stand aside, she is now under our command."

The Mother Abbess knew that she could do no more. Even if her jurisdiction was great enough to take charge, she knew that the strength of the men was greater. Within her she knew that this had no right to take place in the Order she belonged to, but times were changing and the rights of nuns and monks were no longer considered in the same way.

Suddenly I felt my habit being ripped away from my body and my flesh was revealed. The men tore at my garments, fresh ones I had just been given by the Mother Abbess. "Look for the mark of the devil on this witch and harlot," shouted the man whom I feared.

There I stood totally shamed and humiliated, as naked as I had ever been, as both body and soul were exposed at the same time. My sacred vessel of the Lord was now defiled as these men with rough hands prodded, pushed and humiliated me in front of my beloved Mother Abbess.

"Tell me of your liaison with the Devil, for the Devil it must be if you deny all other carnal knowledge. Who is the father of this brat? He must also be devilish if not the Devil himself. Confess to your sins, girl! Confess!"

My answer was silence towards them, but in my head I was screaming aloud. "I will not tell. I will never tell. I will not tell his name."

"Where is the offspring," the evil one shouted. "We must have it. It is an unclean being."

"No!" I heard myself scream out, the first loud utterance from my mouth for so many years. "I beg you. Take me, but do not harm my child. She is innocent and has done no wrong. Can't you see she has only a flaw, which ails both men and beasts at times. It is not through sin, for a newborn child is wholly innocent. If you believe it is sin, which has caused this, then take me and punish me for this sin, but never the child!"

The answer to my words was a blow on the head, which caused me to swoon. I do not remember anything else until I came to. I did not know where I was, but there was movement underneath me and there was great discomfort where I lay. I opened my eyes to find myself still naked, but covered with a meal sack, lying on rough wooden planks; the inside of a cart. The droppings around me led me to understand I was being transported in the same way as a pig or a sheep would be transported. I knew that wherever I was going was not a pleasant place.

The journey was an arduous one and cold. I was exposed to the blasts of wind and sleet and all I had to protect me was the rough meal sack. It seemed unending, but my fear kept me going throughout. I tried to pray, but my fears for my child were so great I could not let go. At length I returned to that place within, the place of that heavenly light, where I saw myself and Madeleine together and once again encompassed by the most beautiful light. It was fortunate that I had taken this light with me, as the dark place I was about to enter would need all of this light.

The Prison

As a young child I had once been taken to the town of Saumur by my father and mother to attend a gathering of family. I remembered it well, as it was a happy occasion, one of the only I can remember from my childhood and the years long gone. I knew exactly where I was now headed. The dungeons of the castle at Saumur were infamous. It was here people, innocent or guilty, were thrown to their plight of darkness, dank and fearsome cold and an existence no one upon this earth would wish upon his neighbour.

As the cart swayed and juddered along the road I could hear shouts from the castle wardens, those men who allowed people in and out. I realised that I was being taken to the lower areas of the castle, the area where the dungeons and prison cells were located. I was beyond fear now and felt that if my Maker was ready to welcome my soul, I too was ready. The loss of my daughter gave me no hope. I knew my crime was too great in the eyes of the Lord and that giving birth to a freak of nature was punishment for my sins. This I knew on an earthly level, but in my heart and deep in my soul I knew I had only fulfilled what I had come for: to experience love, true physical and spiritual love, love, which surpasses all else. I knew that I had experienced this love and I hoped that the deepest part of my beloved, Daniel, felt the same. For all his lack of concern and denial of our love, I felt that somewhere within him he still felt the same. This suddenly gave me the hope I needed to carry on and I took a deep breath and remembered – I remembered the forest, I remembered the foliage around me and the sun filtering through the trees. I remembered the sounds, I remembered it all; that sunshine within alit my heart and soul anew.

With head held high, I gathered the filthy meal sack around my body in order to preserve my dignity and I walked into the prison, with the memory of our love in my heart, as if I was a princess in a beautiful gown, stepping in silken slippers onto the ornate steps of the castle, instead of a humiliated, desperate, heartbroken shell of a human being.

Being at the bottom of the pit where life truly feels as though there is no light nor movement ever available is also a very fortuitous place to be, for it allows us at a soul level to take stock of the being we truly are without any frills or furbelows or whatever we call the drama, which is our life story. We are aware of the soul that is the true being and what it has to learn and to contribute within this show, this play, we are at present dancing through. The soul does not make judgement on the raiment worn at present, nor does it look down on itself and compare itself with the person playing the part in the drama, which appears to cause everyone to shun them. No, instead the soul grasps the knowledge of what is truly happening in the drama and can see each character individually and what they represent in the learning the soul itself has sought to make available to itself.

Perhaps the knowledge of this helped me to be a watcher, rather than a judge. I watched, as it seemed, from afar, when the jailers pushed me into the most dark and dismal cell. I watched from afar as they jeered at me and prodded me making lewd suggestions, although they too were cloaked in disgust for the being I was. I watched all of this as if on a high plateau, being aware of what was happening in the foreground, but not being there. I seemed able to cast off the horror of the situation and to be able to both accept it and understand it. The taunts, the physical pain and the indignities seemed to belong to another person, albeit one whose feelings and thoughts I could access, but which I could turn away from and allow to drop off me.

My belief that I had played out this tale in order to attain a higher level of understanding was always at the forefront and thus I was able to survive. I believe that survival comes not from the physical body, but from the belief within the soul that there is a place beyond the one we inhabit while on earth. I believe that the soul can survive great depravity and lack if on an inner level it dwells in a paradise beyond that of this earthly plane. I knew that the days and weeks spent in that sad and haunted place, the prison at Saumur, passed by as if in a dream, as I was somewhere else in a place of beauty, wonder and complete love. I knew that whatever happened to me I had nothing to fear, for when at last I left this world all that I could ever wish for awaited me.

Heaven awaits us all the time, but allows us our own time to decide when it is time to go "home". It is already determined when we will leave this earth plane and that moment of time exists within us all. We can hang on to life in miserable circumstances for many reasons. Often, due to the love we have for those we are to leave behind, we continue on experiencing sadness, loss, regrets, guilt and all manner of deep emotion until such time we become aware that our own learning is complete and that future learning or experience is not necessary. It is at this point we choose to let go and accept that we have done all that we can do.

For those looking on from the earthly plane it can be very difficult to ascertain how we make this decision, but we are led to do it by those who love us so greatly on the other side of the veil. It is they who beckon and call upon us, who strive to catch our attention and to remind us of our contract, remind us of our passage back to the light of "home". When we experience trauma and fear, we lose contact with those beloved souls who await us and who hold us and guide us all the way.

Time was running out just like the sand runs through one's hands. We watch with trepidation as it trickles swiftly through the light of our understanding, not realising that it is we who create this thing called "time". If we only understood that in the realm of human consciousness time is a commodity we ourselves make into a reality. That reality is so misunderstood, as we do not realise that time is a belief, a belief that we are only alive on this earth for such a short time and then it passes. It is such a false belief, as just as we live and breathe in one human form, we can live in another human form at the same time, in another country, in another body, as a man instead of a woman. We are, literally, players in the theatre of the universe, small perhaps in our own eyes, but in the huge vastness of the universe, great parts, all who are needed to create what makes the whole just that: a whole.

Perhaps when the time comes closer to our

leaving this earthly world, we begin to see life from a different angle. We let go of the chains that bind us and hold us fettered and unable to connect with that place we call "home". Every human soul is aware of this place, although many spend lifetimes denying that such a place exists. In denying "Home", we deny our own identity and in doing so we carry on the eternal cycle of pain and suffering. Why, oh why do we dismiss our true reality? If only we could retain this understanding how much easier would life be? If, however, we did remember in each life, would we be able to push ourselves through the deep and painful learning curves we move through?

The sound of chains rattling in the darkness woke me from a slumber. I was aware that I was being approached by the jailers and I feared the worse. I was, however, not to be singled out for the worst this time. Instead, an elderly lady appeared at my side, followed by the jailer. "Don't be long," he chastised her. "She won't be here much longer. Can't imagine why you would want to spend time with the likes of her..."

By now I was used to the taunts of the jailers and those around me, so I did not react. I was more amazed that someone had come to visit me. The old woman came closer and I thought I remembered her face as one of the village people, who came to the Abbaye at times bringing produce for the nuns.

"I have been sent by the Mother Abbess," she said slowly. "She wishes me to give you her blessing and to know that the nuns are praying for your soul. She would have wanted to come herself, but there was no way she could be seen here. There is great turbulence in the Abbaye after what happened with you. It has resulted in great difficulties for all of the other nuns. Mother Abbess does not chastise you for this, as she knows that it is a way for the church authorities to take her leadership from her. She asked me to tell you this. I am not involved in the daily workings of the Abbaye, but I understand enough to see what is happening with my own eyes. I do not judge you, but instead I have pity for your impossible situation. I have brought you some food to help you in these last days. I know that it won't be long before you meet your Maker and I would want you to know that there are those of us who care about you and abhor what has happened. You treated my husband once and restored his health and for that I am forever grateful. Please accept this humble repast. God be with you and may He hold you in His hand. Your little daughter will be cared for. She is well hidden and I know that she thrives. Do not fret on her account."

The old woman held her hand on my arm, patted my cheek and then turned round and walked quickly to the door of the cell. Her presence and the calm she left with her caused me to feel nurtured and loved. I knew that despite all that was happening to me I was safe and looked after. I was not alone in the world, nor forgotten, but thought of and cherished. The knowledge that Madeleine also was safe helped me greatly. I knew that I could survive now through whatever awaited me knowing that she was safe and would remain so. My life was over, the short time I had been on this earth, but it had taught me a great thing. I had been able to communicate with God and my beloved Jesus throughout and knew that I was a worthy being. I had expressed the greatest love anyone could ever wish for and I had given birth to a darling child. I had also had the joy of helping others through darkness, pain and trauma and for this I would always be grateful. I had left small marks upon this earth, but still, marks they were.

* * *

"Blessed are the meek, for they shall inherit the Earth," it is told in the Holy Bible. This one beautiful phrase ran through my thoughts hour after hour in that dark and dank place. For some reason this had come to me in these last days to give me strength. Knowing that I was still worthy through my belief that we all inherit another "Earth" if we hold our vision secure and untainted, I could cope with the fears of what was to happen to me.

It was not to be many days until a dawn broke bringing a thin sunlight into the sky. There was the sense of rain in the air and a feeling of closure, as if the seasons were merging into one another and there was hope of renewal at hand. Perhaps I alone felt this, as I sensed that my life on this Earth was about to end.

I had been alone throughout my imprisonment in the jail at Saumur, but that morning I was to meet others, who awaited the same fate as myself. I was alone in what I had done to deserve to be incarcerated in this place, but there were others just as unfit to be held here as I. There were children, whose only crime had been to be orphaned and left with no means to survive. Hunger brings about the need to steal to survive. There were women cast aside as harlots, whose only crime was that they had been spurned by their husbands and found comfort elsewhere. There were so many sad fates in that dreadful prison, fates that could have been turned around by one word of love and compassion, but it was not to be.

It is a very different understanding of judgement we encounter on this Earth, as compared to what judgement means in the spheres of Light. Judgement there, means only that we judge ourselves of being worthy of less love than is available to us at all times. How sad it is that we have misunderstood the true meaning and reality behind it on this Earth. True judgement is only in the eyes of ourselves in judging ourselves.

As I was pushed out of the cell and through more cells into the light of day. I asked for the light of God to be spread to those suffering in this great darkness. Seeing that my fate was no worse than many others was strangely comforting.

As I came out into the thin sunlight I was horrified

to see a crowd of people awaiting my appearance.. There was a cheer as I appeared, but the voices I heard shouting were hurling insults and profanities at me and not words of encouragement. Thankfully I had, at some point in my stay in the prison, been given a shift of nondescript material to wear, in order to keep some warmth in my body. I was so glad to have this now and not to be exposed completely. It was enough to feel that my inner self was totally exposed.

At the front of the crowd I saw the face of what I call "the perpetrator of evil". It was the man, who had tried to take my child away. He was dressed in his formal robes as a man of authority in the community and I could see that underneath the covering of his station was a weak and lost soul. Perhaps his path through life had been less than happy and he had found a way around this by assuming a great sense of power. Often if we peel away the layers around people we become aware of the reality which causes them to react the way they do. Who could know what fear or sadness lay at the root of this man's behaviour. At this time I could feel only pity for him in the role he had to play.

My eyes fell on several people in the crowd, as I scanned around to see if there was anyone I might recognise. There were several faces I recognised from my days before the Abbaye, the days of childhood and innocence. They were perhaps there to represent my parents, who I know could not be here.

It had been brought to my attention, while in the Abbaye, that my mother had developed a sickness, which caused her much pain and an inability to stand for any period of time. I assumed that the journey would have been too great for her to endure, not least the torture it would have caused her to see her daughter put to death. My father's absence I would have expected, as his world was always to do with his standing and the acceptance of others. To stand in front of his disgraced daughter – a nun and a daughter of Christ – would be far too much for him to even contemplate, whether or not it might bring his daughter some comfort and acceptance in her last moments.

As I stood there with cold fear cloaking my heart and mind, my eyes strayed to the edge of the crowd, towards the back. My heart leaped and I wanted to shout out loud, for my eyes met the bluest eyes I had ever encountered. The bluest eyes I could never forget. There in the crowd stood Daniel ; he had come to support me in this the most dreadful situation I found myself in. As I caught his gaze, time stood still and I could feel his thoughts and his emotions in that moment. He was not wearing his cassock, but had hidden behind peasant clothes and a peasant's hat. It mattered not to me that he did not have the strength to show himself as a priest, it mattered only that he had come. He had chosen to show me that he loved me, as much as I loved him. My heart swelled over with love for him and I knew that I had to be careful in order to protect him in the crowd. If I stared too long, people would soon start to look as to where I was gazing.

Realising this, Daniel moved towards a building, in order that he be concealed more easily. I could not look away knowing he was there. His presence was to hold me up throughout the dreadful moments, which were to follow. As if in a different space I heard people shouting and words being thrown towards me. I was being dealt out my fate by the words of the authorities. I had sinned as a witch, a daughter of Christ, who had besmirched her standing and in so doing besmirched the face of God. Not only that, I had given birth to what would only be deemed as a devil. My Madeleine had the mark of the devil, they said, due to her disfigurement. I heard the words shouted out as if in a dream. I, whose only crime was that of loving and loving in the wrong way in the eyes of the world around me. I was now being treated as an object rather than a human being. I had no worth, no words to be heard and no means of asking for pardon. This was truly the end.

At that I was thrust forward to a stake, which had been prepared for me to be tied to. My hands were brutally pulled behind my back and I was bound with thick rope. I heard the cry from ahead, shouting, "Kill the witch, kill the witch!" The crowd became boisterous and angry and pushed forward in order to communicate their disgust and loathing. People spat at me and threw old vegetables. I stood there in the sight of God and instead of the pathetic figure I could have been, I became the strength within me and I stared into Daniel's eyes. I knew he was here to help me die, to help my mortal soul to pass over into the realms of the everlasting.

He held my gaze throughout, his strength holding me up when my breast was bared and the sword brought forward to slice the witch into pieces. He held me up as I prayed to the angels who I now saw surround me, lighter and more glorious than I could ever have envisaged. Daniel held my gaze as my soul flew out of my body and up into the spheres of light and I felt a release such as I could never have expected. The love I was sent by this man was so great it gave me strength to accept my fate and to follow the path of the angels, who led me into a place of peace and love, a place filled with the Divine. My fears of death in the earthly plane were over. The pain I had feared was gone, not even a memory. I was a glorious, shining being, fine and resplendent as the soul I was.

As I left my body to go with the angels, the last words I heard in my heart were "I love you.". I knew they came from Daniel and were sent from his heart to mine. I knew then I was free and able to move on to celestial climes, ready to review my life and to take stock of what I had learned and what I had still yet to learn. I knew that there was a huge bond still between Daniel and I. I knew all of this as if by some kind of inner magic. I was and yet I was not. I was myself, Cecile de Martin, but also something greater. I was no longer of flesh, but of a lightness that bore no resemblance to anyway I had ever felt. I was at total peace, floating, as if a feather was being propelled by a very light breeze. I floated and floated in total bliss.

As I floated along I became aware of other bodies of light, who floated along with me. I was aware of them, but there was no interaction. There seemed to be no need for such. We were all in total bliss as we floated, propelled by love. We floated as if we were being pulled in a direction, which we knew we would reach at last. Each of us was aware and yet we had no need for awareness. It was enough to know we were being steered by love. Memory ceases to be a word used now in this realm of true contentment and as I tell my story now it is from another dimension. Suffice it to say we all come to this place at some time. Some of us reach this place sooner or quicker than others, depending on the story of their lives.

This is, thus, my story; the story I have needed to tell for such a long, long time. This is my story of one small time on earth, one time as the being Cecile de Martin. I am, however, not only she, but many, many other identities with so many names. I have told my story through the identity, which I now possess and it has been a cathartic experience for us both. We are not separate beings, but the same soul in a different experience. The soul within is the same, putting together experiences in order that they come into one complete story in the end. What we come to experience is often what we already have experienced, but have not fully accomplished in one life. Perhaps now through my voice and the voice of my writer, my message can be told to a world, which is perhaps more ready to receive it. The two epochs in history have been very similar, the mediaeval times of great religious wonder filled with angels, religious fervour and a need to connect to the being we call God. It is apparent now, in this age, often called, the New Age, where angels once again play a great part and the connection with the source of all things is now worshipped in many, many ways and humanity can worship as they choose; at least in a great many more areas of the world than in my day. There is hope, great hope for the future if only man will awaken to what is always there: the Divine within. If this story can somehow allow this to happen, then my small part in the whole play of life will have been worth it. My message is very simple: it is that we are love, purely and simply. We are here to be that love throughout our earthly days; to cherish and love one another and to learn from all experiences that love is all we need to know.

It is time now to return to that wonderful, life giving dance, the sun dance. To twirl, to look up to the sun and to receive the wondrous energy from that blissful source. Now is the time for my dance to end and another to begin...

Epilogue to Cecile

I started writing this story around 1998. It was a strange sequence of events, which started the process. I had attended a workshop on past lives and had a very traumatic experience. I was led by the workshop leader to a life as a nun and was told I had been raped by a priest. I remember being on my knees and hearing this strange wailing coming from somewhere, as if it was someone else. The words uttered were, "The shame, the shame..." I realised that the voice crying out was my own and yet not my own. The workshop leader's voice was somewhere in the background telling the group that this was not made up, but raw emotion.

This started something deep within me and some weeks later I decided to try to my hand at inspirational writing. I had read about this, but had never attempted it. The result was quite beautiful and very profound. Spurred on by this first attempt, I started to write again and was amazed to read, "It is the summer of 1497..." I was so surprised I couldn't stop writing. The words formed onto the page without any need for thought and within a short while I had filled almost two A4 pages. Reading back what I had written, I was stunned. The words on the page seemed to tie in with the experience I had had at the past life workshop. Where were these words coming from?

Over the next few weeks and months I was drawn more and more into the life of Cecile, whose voice this was. I had been "told", while writing, that the story had taken place in France. I set off for the local library (long before Google made this all so easy), to find some books on France and to perhaps find a clue as to where the story had unfolded. I had an inner trust that somehow I had to write this story in order to help this person called Cecile. I had no real knowledge of past lives, but I had a deep sense that I was being used for some reason. I had been on a spiritual path for some time, learning more about life as a soul on this Earth and our purpose while we are here. I had a sense that whatever was flowing through me would help me in this process.

The first book I opened about France flew open

at a page giving information on the Loire Valley, somewhere I had never been. There was a picture of the Abbaye de Fontevraud. I read the information and whilst reading found myself shaking and feeling very emotional. It seemed I had found my answer.

In the days following, the writings told more of Cecile's life as a nun and how she came to be in the Abbaye. I found that the words which came through often felt as if they had been translated, as sometimes they were a little stilted in English, but still seemed to flow beautifully. Each time I sat down to write I was so excited, as I never knew what would flow from my pen. Soon after I started writing I had a sense of what had happened in Cecile's life, that is to say the end result, but I did not know how events were to play out. There were times over the many years it took me to complete the story, when I left a sentence unfinished, only to pick it up, mid-sentence, months later. It was so simple and easy to write, yet I could not understand why I had to push myself to write the story.

During the years I have been writing the story, I have met people who are in my life at the moment, who also had memories of that life. It seems strange, but it is the truth. When recounting my experiences of Cecile's story, I often found that people would have the same reactions as I did and sense a shiver or an emotional reaction. Often they would quite clearly see the pictures I was seeing in my head to do with what was happening in the story at that time.

Over the years of writing I have met the Mother Superior, a jailer in the prison at Saumur, Columbine, several of the nuns, "the perpetrator of evil" and Daniel, himself. It is not easy meeting someone you recognise so well and with the emotion attached, and this is why we normally do not remember our past incarnations, as they can truly play havoc with the life we are in at this time. I am grateful that we were able to pass each other on our individual journeys, as it confirmed for me that the soul does come back many times and that emotions survive the turning of time. It is sometimes too overwhelming to experience such long gone emotion when it reaches us many centuries later.

My good friend, the artist Jo Abbott encountered Cecile whilst I was giving Jo Reiki. This took place at the time I was receiving the deepest parts of the story. At the session's end, Jo opened her eyes and said, "I have just seen a pregnant nun" – and not long after, she painted the image from that encounter. I am very grateful that Jo has allowed this painting to grace, and to complete, the book upon its front cover.

In writing Cecile's memories I have realised that my life has been a mirror of her life. This now explains why it took me so long to finish what is in essence a short story. It seemed, however, that I was experiencing in my own life a mirroring of the situation Cecile found herself in. I do not mean by that, mediaeval torture, but similar lessons being learned.

Cecile became a huge part of my life and always will be. She has taught me so much not least about myself. It seems I have been blessed with the ability to access past lives easily. I say blessed, but this can be a curse at times. It has, however, taught me so much about the continuation of the soul and how we do not necessarily live only one life at a time. There is a belief that time is a continuum and events are taking place in the past, the present and the future all at the same time. I feel comfortable with this way of thinking and it has helped me to understand my connection with Cecile de Martin. We are at root, one and the same being, living as different individuals in different times, but always the same soul. Perhaps we will merge even more as we continue dancing on in the evolution of the soul.

About Alison

Having started to write through inspiration, I am now an article writer for Sibyl Magazine, an online spiritual magazine for women. I will be submitting inspirational articles for Sibyl once a month during 2016. I have also been writing a second remembered story, following the life of a young woman and her family. The story has no definite country nor time, but as it unfolds it will no doubt become clear where it might be. I have deliberately not given information around this, as I am once again writing down what "the voice" writes. As this story could be happening again all around us, it is more about the human condition and how we treat each other as human beings, in ways which are inconceivable, if we were to view ourselves as souls who are in essence love.

If you would like to contact Alison after reading the story of Cecile, please visit her website at www.alisonstrandberg.co.uk.

The Forgotten Stars

A long time ago in a small village on the outskirts of a large and beautiful city there lived a family in a small house, surrounded by trees. In summer the birds sang in the trees all day long and in winter the family decorated the branches of the trees with food for the birds as the snow fell and food for them became scarce. The birds stayed close to the house all year round, some leaving to return at different times of the year and others staying and almost becoming a part of the family. The birds seemed to represent safety, security and a sense that time flows, but closeness and trust are always there, no matter what may happen.

The family lived frugally, but with great care for each other. The mother loved her children so much she could be as fierce as a lioness if any of them ever came close to the slightest danger. In this little house of safety and calm, where troubles were like the heads of dandelions and could always be blown away, this sense of protective ferocity could seem somewhat misplaced, but it was there and some day in a future far ahead it would be awakened and she would fight tooth and nails for her little ones.

The family consisted of a mother, father, and three small children, two little boys and a little girl. The little boys were very devoted to their sister, who was the youngest of the children. She was a fragile little thing and had been very small when first born and thus the family had had to allot extra care to her well-being from the time of her arrival. She was, however, a strong and very brave person within herself and the waif-like outer appearance hid a great and deep sense of self. She possessed the same quality as her mother; the quality of fighting for what was dear to her and for any situation that seemed to her unfair, either to herself or to any other living being. Her sense of nurturing was great and although her brothers were older and seemed to be in the role of protectors towards her, she was in essence the protector for them with the inner light and fire, which lit her up from within.

The little girl had a depth within her, which shone through her eyes and caused people to stop at times and contemplate upon what they had just experienced. It was as if she was the source of a fire or a light that lit up other people from within. Others became aware of a shift in themselves when she looked at them, as if she could see deep within their hearts and souls and knew who they really were and what their destiny was. The little girl, whose name was Anna, was not always aware of this innate ability and at times found it hard to be singled out by people, who came to her as if drawn to a light. This inner ability was so much part of her she could not understand why others were drawn to this aspect of her, as she was of the belief that all people had the same ability. Fortunately Anna's mother could understand what was happening, as she, too, possessed the same ability, although less defined, and she could help her daughter in situations, which caused her discomfort.

Anna's mother, Milenka, had grown up in a family, who were not always comfortable with the feelings that surfaced when Milenka's inner light shone forth onto troubled areas and they had taught her that her ability was to be hidden and not encouraged. Seeing the power in Anna helped Milenka to understand the sadness and pain this had caused her as a young girl and was anxious that this would not affect her own child. She wanted Anna to be safe, trouble-free and to nurture this gift, which she possessed, but in a way that would not damage her in any way.

Anna's father, Isak, whose family name was Pasha, was the strength in the family, but in a different way. He was also a person of great depth and great fairness, but he did not possess the more ethereal qualities of his wife and daughter. His sense of fairness was grounded in a respect for his fellow man, in that life is a gift we are given and given to share with our fellow human beings in the most positive way. He was a man of honour and thus expected the same of others and had been fortunate enough in life not to have had to face too many difficulties in this area of life. In showing respect, respect was reciprocated and life then maintained its equilibrium. In the same way that his wife, Milenka, possessed the fiercely protective energy, which was there, but mostly dormant, his issues to do with honour and respect not being reciprocated were also to be challenged in a harsh and cruel way. Who would have known this in the light of the life the family lived. Who could have foreseen what was to come...

Made in the USA
Charleston, SC
03 November 2016